4⁰⁰

The Desert

The Desert

John Cloudsley-Thompson

G. P. Putnam's Sons · NEW YORK

Frontispiece: Death Valley, California (Marka)
Endpapers: Agave and prickly pear in the Great American Desert (Marka)

© Orbis Publishing Limited, London
and Istituto Geografico de Agostini S.p.A, Novara 1977
SBN: 399-11885-3
Library of Congress Catalog Card Number: 76-28655
Printed in Italy by IGDA, Novara

Contents

The Wilderness

The rise of technology has changed the face of the earth. It has led to enormous increases in the possession of material goods and to the squandering of the world's resources at an unprecedented rate. Those natural resources on which we depend are energy, minerals, soil, water, air, plants and animals, but we tend to assess them in an absurdly materialistic way. We regard land that is unproductive in economic terms as being 'wasteland', forgetting that, in its natural state, it may be beautiful, scientifically interesting, or merely the home of native plants and wild animals.

We are also apt to forget the enchantment of solitude, the exhilaration of open spaces, the satisfaction of self-reliance. The desert provides an abundance of both, and has inspired many a poet and artist.

'Oh! that the desert were my dwelling place,
    With one fair spirit for my minister, . . .'
wrote Lord Byron (*Childe Harold*, IV). Oliver Goldsmith (*The Deserted Village*) was, perhaps, less appreciative of wilderness:

'Those poisonous fields with rank luxuriance
    crowned
Where the dark scorpion gathers death around;
Where at each step the stranger fears to wake
The rattling terrors of the vengeful snake.'

Over 18 per cent of the earth's land surface is occupied by tropical and subtropical desert and semi-desert, much of which has been created by human activity. This area is expanding annually at an alarming rate due to misuse of the environment. For this reason, a study of the ecology of deserts is important, for it confers an understanding of the factors that create them. To the scientist, however, the solution of biological problems for their own sake is often more exciting than the

Left: The Atacama desert, Antofagasta province, Chile, with the Andes mountains in the background. The pass of Huaitiquina which leads into Argentina is clearly visible.

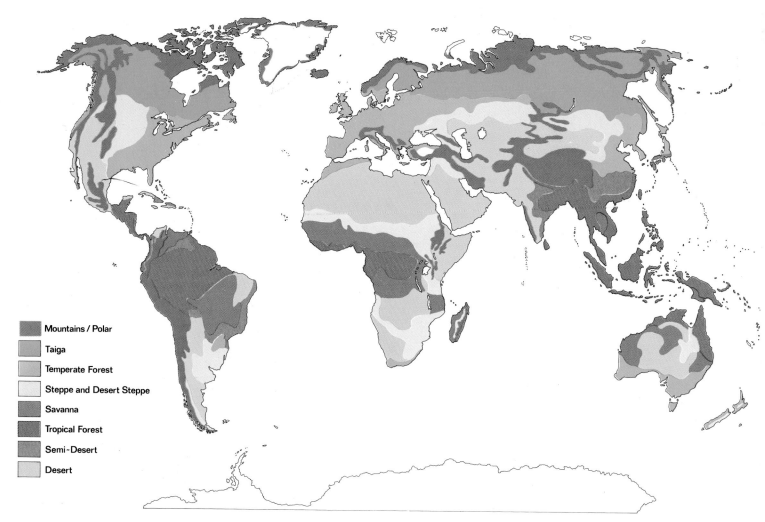

Mountains / Polar

Taiga

Temperate Forest

Steppe and Desert Steppe

Savanna

Tropical Forest

Semi-Desert

Desert

practical application of the knowledge gained, and the adaptation of plants and animals to life in arid regions provides a rewarding subject for basic research.

Desert regions are not necessarily characterized by great heat, nor do they always consist of vast expanses of shifting sand dunes. Indeed, polar deserts rarely experience temperatures in excess of 10°C (50°F). The one characteristic common to them all is their aridity throughout most or all of the year. When the air is humid, not only does less solar heat penetrate to the ground during the day, but less is lost from the earth by radiation at night. Consequently, humid climates tend to show daily or seasonal stability, while deserts are characterized by extremes of temperature and humidity. The most adverse conditions for life consist of a combination of aridity and high or low temperatures, and it is the effects of these two factors that have been studied most extensively. The combination of drought and high temperature presents an unusually acute thermoregulatory challenge to warm-blooded animals, because it poses the singularly intractable problem of losing heat to a hot environment while simultaneously keeping water-loss to a minimum.

Although superficially very different from tropical and subtropical deserts, the Arctic and polar deserts resemble them in one very important way: the annual season of growth is extremely short. It is not by chance that both are desert wastelands. In tropical and subtropical deserts the plants, upon which all animal life ultimately depends, only grow when rain has fallen. This rain can come from a single thunderstorm after years of drought, or it may occur sporadically during a limited rainy season. In polar deserts, on the other hand, although water is present throughout the year it is frozen and therefore not available to plants and animals except during the brief summer. In either event, vegetation is scarce and animals are faced with a shortage of food. This is particularly significant in polar regions where animals need a considerable amount of food in order to generate enough heat to counter the winter's bitter cold. In all, polar deserts extend over nearly as much of the earth (16 per cent of the land surface) as do tropical and subtropical deserts, but polar deserts are practically uninhabited.

Arctic climates are of two types, *tundra* climates with a short summer when the temperature rises above freezing, and polar, or perpetual frost, climates. Polar climates are found

Above: Map showing the world's principal terrestrial biomes – climatic/vegetational environments.

Above right: The sandy desert, known as erg, in Libya, with tufts of perennial grass and small barchan dunes.

Right: The coast of Terre Adélie, the French territory in Antarctica, in summer. Small floes are breaking off from the ice sheet in the foreground, while barren rock projects through the ice beyond. In winter the entire landscape is covered with a deep layer of snow.

8

throughout most of the Antarctic continent. The growth of vegetation in tundra is possible during the short period of each year in which the ground is free from snow but, in regions of perpetual frost, the growth of vegetation is almost impossible. Tundra, a word of Finnish origin, means an open, forestless stretch of country. It is applied to the huge tract of land which lies north of the Arctic Circle, but which thaws briefly in summer. In the southern hemisphere, the tapering of the land masses makes the development of true tundra impossible. Typical tundra is treeless, but there are patches of stunted coniferous forests in the valleys of rivers such as the Lena and Yenisei, and along the coasts of northern Russia. These, however, are really outliers of the *taiga*, that vast region of coniferous forest which lies to the south of the tundra. In this book we shall use the term 'polar desert' to include regions that experience both tundra and polar climates. This will avoid confusion because 'cold desert' is frequently applied to subtropical deserts that suffer cold winters even though the summers are hot. The Gobi desert in Mongolia, and the Patagonian desert in Argentina provide good examples of this.

Tropical and subtropical, and polar deserts

form two of the world's major terrestrial environments or 'biomes'. Before considering them in detail, it is worthwhile reviewing them with other biomes, so that they are seen in perspective.

The major climatic regions of the world, and the principal types of vegetation they support are summarized in the table at the end of this chapter. From this, it can be seen that the type of vegetation found in any particular region of the world depends primarily on temperature and rainfall. In a journey from the equator to the Poles, the ambitious traveller would pass through the world's principal terrestrial biomes as follows:

Tropical forest A vast girdle of rain-forest encircling the earth between the tropics enjoys a humid tropical climate in which the average daily range of temperature exceeds by several times the difference between the warmest and coolest months of the year. The sun's rays are never far from vertical, and day lengths vary little throughout the year. The abundance of cloud and dense forest prevents excessive temperatures and the climate is characterized by its uniformity and monotony. There is little seasonal change and the differences between day and night are less marked than in open country.

Savanna Park-like savanna-woodlands are found where the dry season is longer and the rainfall less than in regions of tropical forest. Precipitation is variable, with the rainy season usually being ushered in and out by violent thunderstorms and wind squalls alternating with extremely hot sunshine. Flora and fauna are dominated by the seasons: in the absence of marked changes in day length and temperature, the pronounced division of savanna climate into wet and dry seasons is the main meteorological factor affecting the environmental physiology of savanna animals.

Tropical and subtropical desert The world's greatest deserts lie beyond the limits of the annual swing of the equatorial rainfall belt, at the latitudes in which the trade winds blow throughout the year, where the annual precipitation is below 25.5 cm (10 ins). Hot deserts, such as the Sahara and Kalahari, have no cold season but, in 'cold deserts', like the Gobi and Great Basin, one or more of the winter months has a mean temperature below 6°C (43°F). Aridity, rather than high mean temperatures, is the most characteristic feature of the desert. Desert climates are subject to extremes. High temperatures with low humidity during the day are followed by comparatively cold nights. Long periods of drought are broken by torrential rainfall and flooding and, although desert rainfall tends to be seasonal, it is most erratic and unreliable.

Right: Short grass in the arid foothills of the Pamir Mountains, east of Tashkent.

Steppe Temperate grasslands occupy the interiors of the continents in temperate regions where the summers are hot, the winters cold, and the annual rainfall low. Only on the shores of lakes and along the banks of rivers is there usually sufficient moisture for trees to grow.

Temperate forest This may take many forms depending on the climatic regions. In cooler latitudes the trees are mainly deciduous, but evergreens predominate in warmer regions. The three main types are: temperate deciduous, moist temperate coniferous and broad-leaved deciduous forest.

Taiga This is a form of coniferous forest which exists in regions where the growing season is too short to support deciduous woodlands. Because they are evergreen, coniferous trees are ready to begin photosynthesis without delay as soon as temperatures become favourable. Moreover, coniferous trees have the advantage in that they pollinate one year and the seeds are dispersed the next, whereas deciduous trees have to complete the process in a single season. Length of growing season, with temperatures above the threshold for growth, is clearly the most significant factor controlling forest types.

Polar deserts The inequality of the length of day and night reaches its maximum at the Poles. Insolation (exposure to the sun's rays) is absent in winter and continuous in summer. Tundra vegetation is exposed to extremely adverse circumstances which eliminate all but a few hardy species. A long period of frost is followed by an extremely short growing season and most of the

Above: Sand dunes of the Grand Erg Occidental (Great Western Erg) near Timimoun in central Algeria. The action of the wind has sculptured the dunes and covered their surfaces with smaller ripples.

WORLD CLIMATES AND VEGETATION

Climate	Vegetation
Mountain regions: dependent on latitude and altitude	
Desert regions: low rainfall	
hot: no month below 6°C (43°F)	scrub
cold: one or more months below 6°C (43°F)	scrub
Arctic regions: no month above 10°C (50°F)	tundra
Cold regions: six or more months below 6°C (43°F)	
marine	taiga
continental or boreal	taiga or steppe
Cool temperate regions: one to five months below 6°C (43°F)	
marine	temperate forest
continental	taiga or steppe
Warm temperate regions (or subtropical): no month below 6°C (43°F)	
western margin	temperate forest
eastern margin	temperate forest
continental	steppe
Hot regions: mean annual temperatures above 21°C (70°F)	
equatorial	rain-forest
tropical marine	rain-forest
tropical continental	savanna

tundra overlies deep deposits of sphagnum, resulting from the failure of dead plants to decompose at low temperatures.

Mountains On account of the low temperatures and short summers, trees do not grow at high altitudes. The Alpine zone above the timberline is in many ways similar to the polar regions. There are certain differences, however. At high altitudes, atmospheric pressure is reduced. Day length is related to latitude rather than to altitude and, at high elevations, the atmosphere is thin. Consequently, insolation is powerful on mountain tops, in contrast to polar regions where the rays of the sun are strongly filtered as they pass obliquely through the atmosphere. Winds reach high speeds because frictional drag with the earth's surface is reduced.

The various macro-environments described above can be classified according to their climates or by topographical features. The topography of the land and the variations of its climate represent the same part in the make-up of the environment, figuratively speaking, as morphology (body form) and physiology (body processes) do in the life of an animal. Thus, irrespective of climate, the mammalian fauna of desert, savanna, steppe, tundra and high plateaux have certain features in common. In each, the dominant forms tend to be either large, fast moving herbivores, or subterranean rodents. The structural adaptations of limbs for running, leaping or digging, are usually similar in unrelated forms from different parts of the world. In contrast, the inhabitants of tropical rain-forest, temperate deciduous forest, and of taiga, tend to show similar adaptations to life in trees. Likewise, flying animals show comparable adaptations, whether they be insects, molluscs, fish, amphibians, reptiles, birds or mammals.

Seasons when conditions are unfavourable may be avoided by migration, which occurs in various groups of the animal kingdom and, with land animals, is especially conspicuous among insects, birds and mammals. Alternatively, dormancy is adopted, and is known as hibernation in winter or as aestivation in summer.

A study of the adaptations of animals to their environment emphasizes the relationship between their morphology, physiology and ecology.

The Desert Environment

The deserts of the world can be divided into five basic types according to climate: subtropical deserts, cool coastal deserts, rain-shadow deserts, interior continental deserts and polar deserts. The first four of these enjoy warm or hot summers and relatively cool winters which, in some cases, may be very cold. Water is deficient throughout most of the year because the amount of evaporation greatly exceeds the annual rainfall. In polar deserts the brief summers are generally cool or cold, and the winters bitterly cold. Although water is present, it is frozen for most of the year, and therefore not readily available to plants and animals.

Weather and climate exist as part of a global system of air movements, and desert areas are often quite small in relation to the wind systems that dominate them. The distribution of low latitude deserts throughout the world is due mainly to the way in which the atmosphere circulates, particularly in its lower layers. Tropical and subtropical deserts are the result of semi-permanent belts of high pressure within which the air tends to sink from high altitudes towards the surface of the land. At the beginning of its descent, this air is cold and dry, but it becomes warmer at the rate of about 10°C per 1000 m (50°F per 3280 ft) as a result of being compressed. Consequently, when it reaches the ground it is very hot and has an extremely low moisture content so that it is incapable of producing any precipitation.

Cool coastal deserts are almost always rainless, yet they are often drenched with chilly moisture: they include the Namib of south-west Africa, Atacama in Chile and Peru and the coastal desert of Baja California. Lack of rain results from

descending air masses, high humidity and coldness from nearby cool ocean currents, respectively the Benguéla, Humboldt and Californian currents. In each case, these currents have originated in polar regions, but they pull up even colder water from the depths which lie near the shores of coastal deserts.

Rain-shadow deserts are situated on the lee sides of mountain ranges which cause the prevailing wind to rise and drop its moisture in the form of rain so that it is dry when it reaches the desert. An example is afforded by the Mojave Desert in California, which owes its winter aridity to the Sierra Nevada and Transverse Ranges, while its aridity in summer is caused by the presence, at that time of the year, of a subtropical high-pressure cell which dominates the Sonoran Desert, California, just to the south. The Great Basin Desert in Nevada is, likewise, sheltered by the Sierra and Cascade Ranges to the west, and by the Rocky Mountains to the east. The deserts of Patagonia, Argentina, are in rain-shadow as far as the prevailing westerly winds from the Pacific are concerned, while air masses moving from the South Atlantic are cooled from the Falkland Islands current and carry little moisture.

The Australian desert is to some extent in the rain-shadow of the Great Dividing Range. Like the Mojave and Great Basin Deserts, however, it also falls into the category of 'continental interior desert', and is arid on account of its distance from the sea and the massive bulk of the land surrounding it. Distance from water is also the final factor in the creation of the deserts of central Asia. The world's largest arid region, the Great Palaearctic deserts, includes the Sahara, Arabian, Iranian, Thar (India), the Takla Makan in China and the

Left : Wind erosion in the Mojave desert of Nevada, USA, which owes its aridity in winter to the Sierra Nevada mountains and in summer to a subtropical high pressure cell which dominates the Sonoran desert to the south.

Below : Dunes of the Atacama Desert at Talara in northern Peru on the coast of the Pacific Ocean. Aridity is caused by the cool Humboldt current.

Right : The Simpson Desert of Australia.

Gobi (Mongolia) deserts which extend almost continuously from the Atlantic coast of North Africa to north-west India and the heart of China.

Although precipitation is low in Arctic and Antarctic regions, there is little evaporation and water accumulates in the form of glaciers and ice-caps. Thus it is frozen for most or all of the year in polar deserts, and therefore not accessible to plants and animals.

Climate

Low latitude desert regions are not necessarily characterized by great heat, nor do they always consist of vast expanses of shifting sand dunes. The only characteristic common to them all is their aridity throughout most, if not all, of the year. Perhaps the most adverse conditions for life consist of a combination of aridity and high temperature.

The climates of deserts are subject to great extremes. High temperatures and low humidity during the day may be followed by comparatively cold nights even in subtropical deserts. Long periods of drought are broken by torrential rainfall and flooding. Although desert rainfall tends to be seasonal, it is most erratic and the total annual precipitation varies considerably from

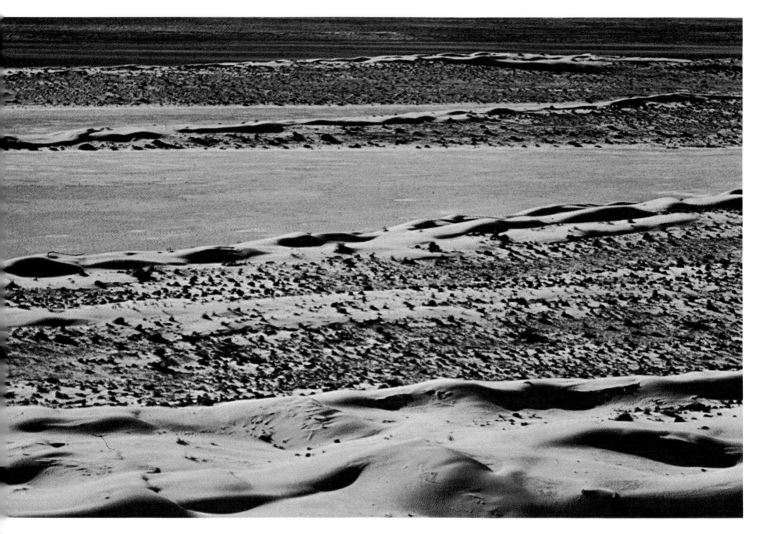

year to year. The presence of dry water courses or *wadis*, and of dry, saline lake beds, such as the *chotts* of North Africa, show that torrential rain may sometimes fall. Most of this rainfall runs off the soil surface quite rapidly, however, and does not therefore provide the moisture essential for plant life.

When the air is laden with water vapour, either diffused or in the form of clouds, not only does less of the sun's heat penetrate to the ground during the day, but less of it is lost by radiation at night. In clear desert air only about 10 per cent of solar radiation is deflected by dust particles and cloud so that 90 per cent reaches the ground. In humid regions, however, some 20 per cent may be deflected by clouds, 10 per cent by dust and a further 30 per cent by water surfaces and vegetation so that only 40 per cent reaches the ground. At night on the other hand, up to 90 per cent of accumulated heat escapes from the desert surface to the upper air while, in humid countries, only 50 per cent escapes, 30 per cent being deflected by clouds and dust, and the remainder being retained by the land cover and water. Consequently, humid equatorial climates tend to show great stability from one day to another and from season to season, whereas deserts are

17

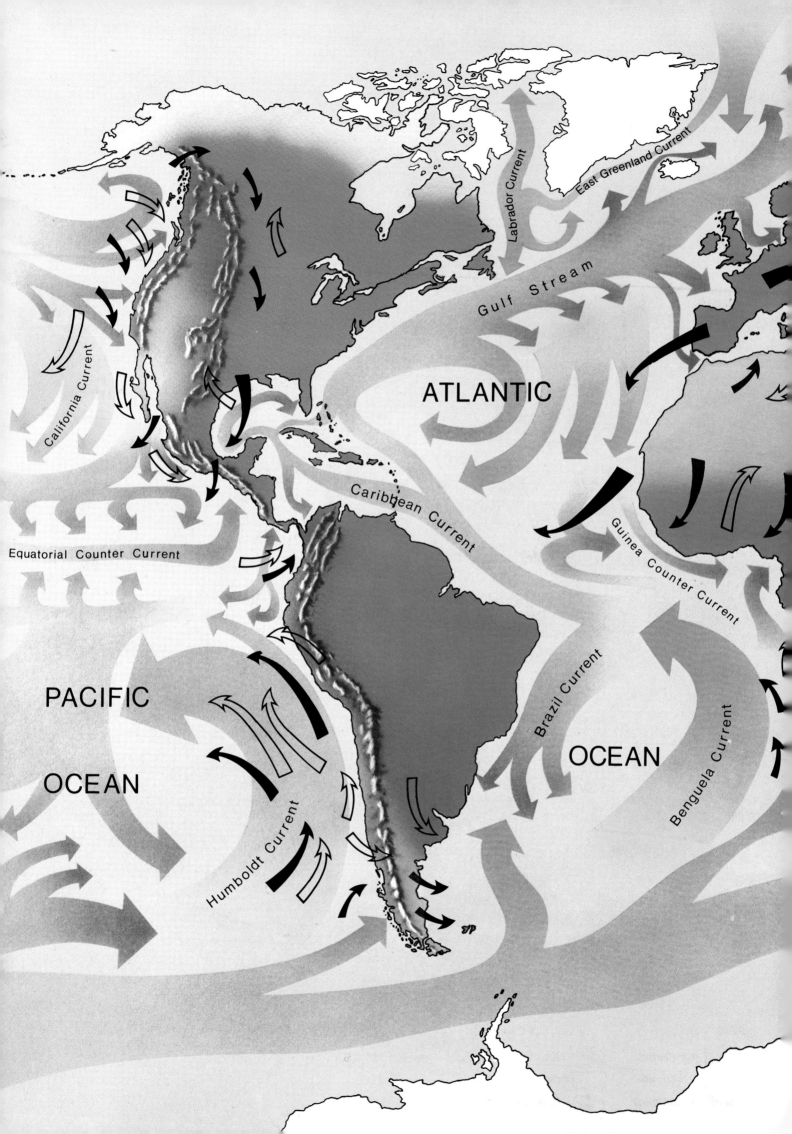

PACIFIC

OCEAN

INDIAN

OCEAN

Kurashio Current

Equatorial Counter Current

Sonalia Current

Agulhas Current

Madagascar Current

West Australian Current

East Australian Current

c Current

Warm Current
Cold Current
January Winds

Desert
Polar Desert
July Winds

Left : A salt lake in the awesome Danaki Desert of Ethiopia, which has been formed as a result of high evaporation.

Below : Salt being prepared by evaporation in the southern Sahara, from where it is taken by camel caravan to Timbuktu.

characterized by extremes of temperature and humidity.

Maximum temperatures are high in low latitude deserts and semi-arid areas, especially in summer. Even in winter, temperatures during daytime are high compared with those of other regions. The mean maximum temperature may reach 43.6°C (111°F) in Baghdad, Iraq, 41.2°C (106°F) in Biskra, Algeria, and 40.0°C (104°F) in Phoenix, Arizona. In cooler arid regions, such as those influenced by cool ocean currents, mean maximum temperatures in summer are considerably lower – for example, 24.4°C (76°F) in Antofagasta in the Atacama desert and 29.4°C (85°F) in Windhoek in south-west Africa. Winter mean maxima are low in the cold interior continental deserts of Asia. At Kashgar in the

Above : Date palms
in southern Morocco.
They are growing in
the bed of a wadi
where they obtain
more moisture than
elsewhere.

Takla Makan desert, for example, the mean maximum is only 0.6°C (33.08°F) in January, while it is as high as 30°C (86°F) in Khartoum on the southern edge of the Sahara.

Mean figures are of little biological significance in deserts, however, because the fluctuations are very great. It is the incidence of high temperatures liable to cause heat damage, and of low temperatures liable to cause frost damage and which limit the growing season of the vegetation, that are important to plants and animals. Shade temperatures as high as 56.5°C (134°F) have been registered in Death Valley, California, and even higher in the Sahara: an annual range of shade temperature from −2°C (28°F) to 52.5°C (126°F) has been recorded from Wadi Halfa, Sudan, and a daily range in summer of 29°C (84°F) at In

Salah, Algeria. The record appears to be a fluctuation of 38°C (100°F) from −0.5°C (31°F) to 37.5°C (99°F), within 24 hours at Bir Mighla in northern Libya in December. During 1910 there were 14 days of frost at Tamanrasset in the Algerian Sahara at an altitude of 1400 m (4593 ft), and absolute minima of −7°C (19.4°F) and −2°C (28.4°F) were recorded.

Not only is lack of rain the chief factor causing desert conditions, but low humidity itself has an adverse effect upon plant and animal life, because the saturation deficiency or evaporating power of the atmosphere increases as temperatures soar during the day. Conversely, there are several examples in low latitudes where a high relative humidity, usually due to dominant onshore winds from the sea, may to a certain degree compensate

Left: A view of Death Valley, California, showing the effect of wind erosion. This part of the Mojave Desert experiences higher temperatures than any other region of the Great American Desert.

for lack of rainfall. In the arid or semi-arid areas along the Persian Gulf, for instance, the vegetation is much better developed than would be expected from rainfall figures, and even includes species characteristic of a more humid tropical flora. As we shall see, animal life in the Namib Desert of south-west Africa depends for its moisture upon fog that comes in from the sea, while food is provided in the form of fragments of dry vegetation blown by the easterly winds of the region.

Strong winds and sandstorms are characteristic of most desert climates, especially in summer. They blow hardest during the day, while the nights are relatively calm. Although their speed seldom exceeds 80 km per hour (50 m.p.h.), and averages over the year only 16 km per hour (10 m.p.h.), the effect is enhanced by the low humidity, high temperature and lack of shelter.

The contrast in polar climates is not between day and night, but between summer and winter. The inequality of the lengths of day and night reaches a maximum near the Poles: diurnal changes are therefore non-existent. Insolation (exposure to the sun's rays) is absent in mid-winter and continuous at midsummer even though the angle of the sun is so low that its feeble rays have little power to melt the snow, which absorbs most of their heat. In the tundra zone of the northern hemisphere, the temperature of the air does not rise above freezing until June and winter sets in by September. Any solid object may, however, be warmed, so that recorded temperatures can exceed 38°C (100°F) even though the air is freezing. Maximum soil surface temperatures of as high as 50°C (122°F) have been recorded at latitude 73°N. Long, bitterly cold winters and short, cool summers are, of course, the rule. Usually only two to four months have average temperatures above freezing, and fatal frosts can occur at any time.

The climate of the tundra is one of the bitterest on earth. In winter, the temperature often drops below −57°C (−71°F). It is not, however, the severity and duration of the cold season as much as the shortness and coolness of the summer that determines the character of the flora and fauna. Then the midday temperature may reach 21°C (70°F) and, although little rain falls, the splash and gurgle of water from the melting snow is heard everywhere. Polar climates have the distinction of producing even colder winters and summers because the rays of the sun are so oblique that they can never be really effective, even during the long summer days. In addition, much of the sun's energy is reflected by the snow and ice, or dissipated in melting the snow, so that

23

neither the land nor the air is warmed. Precipitation is meagre, often less than 25.5 cm (10 ins), but the amount of evaporation is so low that permanent ice-caps have accumulated on Greenland and Antarctica.

The Antarctic, with its great ice-cap, land mass and high mountains, tends to have much colder winters and even cooler summers than the Arctic. Summer temperatures remain consistently below the minimum necessary for the development of most flowering plants and only a very few species are found on the continent of Antarctica, whereas some 400 grow north of the Arctic Circle. In addition, there are abundant mosses and lichens in the Arctic which do not die in winter and are, therefore, permanently available as food for herbivorous animals. This explains the great differences to be observed between the fauna of the two polar deserts.

Recent climatic changes
No account of arid regions in the world today can omit reference to the comparatively recent climatic changes that have taken place. Since the Pliocene epoch, which ended about one million years ago, there have been several ice ages and interglacial periods, whose effects on living organisms, soils and landscapes, are still evident. Even earlier events may also be of direct significance, since fossil soils are still preserved on the present land surface, especially in arid regions. Moreover, many major features of geology and geomorphology (landscape) of current importance were initiated over one million years ago.

Left: Fish River Canyon in the Namib Desert of south-western Africa, one of the oldest deserts in the world.

24

Pluvial periods, during which the rainfall increased in duration and intensity for sufficiently long to be of geological significance, have subsequently occurred at frequent intervals up to the present time. They have affected not only the great desert areas and their margins, but also wide expanses of semi-arid grasslands, from the equator to mid-latitudes. About five million years ago in Africa, shifting desert sands stretched from the Congo River to the Cape. During later periods, the present Kalahari desert, Botswana, has almost disappeared. There have been times when regions of East Africa supported great lakes where, today, even drinking water is unavailable. The Olduvai Gorge of Tanzania, in which have been found the earliest artifacts and cultural traces of man, is one such site.

The most recent series of wet periods began with the onset of the Pleistocene epoch, over one million years ago, when climates changed throughout most of the world. Higher latitudes were subjected to a succession of glacial and interglacial periods while, nearer the equator, an even more complex series of wet and dry periods followed one another. During the ice ages there was a tendency for the rainfall to increase in the interior continental deserts of high latitudes. At such times, the sea-level was lowered by 100 m (328 ft) or more, because so much water was incorporated in the polar ice-caps.

Much of this water was later released during warmer periods when the ice melted and the sea-level rose. Geological traces of such fluctuations in sea-level provide evidence of the various glacial and pluvial periods. Pluvials in the tropics and subtropics cannot, however, be correlated directly with glacial periods in temperate regions of the world. There have been moist, cool intervals in low latitude dry areas, as well as dry, cool intervals, and moist, warm intervals, and dry, warm intervals. In addition, there have been times when there was an ice-cap in the South Atlantic only, and others when there were two polar ice masses. One effect of the northern cap has been to cause the north-east trade winds to blow further south: it has also deflected southward the temperate climate tracks, thus engendering increased rainfall on the northern edge of the Sahara.

During the last interglacial in the Sahara, the climate probably changed from warm and comparatively dry to warm and comparatively moist, while the last glacial period began cool and comparatively moist, afterwards changing to cold and dry. It is believed that the maximum of the last pluvial phase may date back more than 50,000 years and had ended well before the close of the Pleistocene, some 10,000 years ago. The closed Alexandersfontein depression, near Kimberley in South Africa, now only an evaporation pan, contained a lake, 19 m (62 ft) in depth and with a surface area of 44 square km (27.32 square miles), a little over 16,000 years ago. Assuming a temperature depression of 6°C (42.8°F), calculations show that rainfall must have been about double that of today. By 10,000 years ago, however, the climate of the world's arid zones was very similar to today's. Although the climate may have continued to fluctuate slightly, there have been no very marked changes since man's influence on the terrestrial environment first reached significant proportions.

It must always be remembered that the climate in arid regions tends to be very variable, with erratic rainfall. Unusually long, dry periods may therefore result in the destruction of elements of the flora and fauna that have survived since the last wet period. Once this has occurred, there is

very little opportunity for the desert to be subsequently recolonized from less arid areas. Consequently, random climatic variations may have been responsible for the progressive elimination of many ice-cap relics, so that a steady deterioration has taken place quite naturally. This has been greatly accelerated in recent times, however, by bad agricultural practices, the reckless felling of trees, and overgrazing by domestic animals, especially goats.

Landscape

The processes of weathering, erosion and deposition are constantly operating on basic geological structures, destroying old landforms and creating new ones. Such 'physiographic' processes, as they are called, when induced by arid climates give to deserts their consistent appearance – for deserts do not otherwise correspond with any special geological features.

Some deserts rest upon vast sheets of bedrock that have been divided into blocks separated by faults or sharp folds. Large areas of the southwestern United States, including the arid regions, for example, exhibit 'block tectonics'. As a result of differential movements between various blocks of the underlying bedrock, there is a 'basin and range topography', with abrupt escarpments between the upland and lowland regions. Similar structural landforms are found in some parts of the Gobi desert in Mongolia, the Little Kharas mountains of the Kalahari, Botswana, and elsewhere. In contrast, the Sahara is a typical continental platform, a region in which much of

Above: The edge of the sheet ice surrounding the Antarctic continent breaks up when temperatures rise in spring, as shown here in Terre Adélie.

26

the underlying skeleton consists of ancient crystalline and igneous rocks that were subsequently folded and eroded to form a rigid rock shield. The remainder consists of strongly contorted Pre-Cambrian 'basement complex', either exposed or covered with sedimentary rocks. (The Cambrian period, in which the earliest known fossils were laid down, lasted approximately from 510 to 430 million years ago.) Subsequent uprising produced the Hoggar and Tibesti mountains, long before the oldest existing sedimentary rocks were laid down. Arabia is similar to the Sahara, with ranges of rugged mountains on exposed Pre-Cambrian basement rocks while the Australian shield likewise consists of a Pre-Cambrian basement complex bordered by younger rocks. The Thar desert (India and Pakistan) consists of

Above : Hammada – exposed bedrock in the Tassili N' Ajjer region of southern Algeria.

Left : Moving sand is a constant threat to the oases of the Sahara. These palms, growing at El Goléa, Algeria, are endangered by the sands of the Grand Erg Occidental. The oasis of El Goléa lies between the two Algerian ergs.

sand overlying an eroded plain which is interrupted only by occasional low outcrops and ridges. Although the Gobi has high mountains, it also possesses platform characteristics, for there are also large areas of unfolded Mesozoic sediments.

Most of the Sahara was covered by a vast sea throughout much of the Carboniferous period, when the coal measures were deposited. At this time, the sandstone of Adrar and Tassili was deposited. This was followed by a very long period when the land supported huge marshes, lakes and tropical forests, whose fossil remains are associated with those of dinosaurs and other extinct creatures. Sea then covered large areas of the Sahara during the Cretaceous period over 70 million years ago, but there was no continuous

*Above: Rocky
vegetation in the
western Sahara
desert showing the
blackening effect of
'desert varnish'.*

*Above left: The
mountains of Tassili
N' Ajjer near
Djanet in southern
Algeria. Scattered
vegetation can be
seen in the wadi.*

*Left: Desert rainfall
comes in torrential
cloudbursts, seen
here in the Aïr
region of Niger.*

flooding at this time, although the sandstone and limestone of the *hammadas* or rocky soils of Tindouf, Dra and Guir (North Africa) date from that time.

Active volcanoes now tend to be rare in arid regions, but extinct volcanoes are important in several desert landscapes. There are volcanic mountains and lava flows of recent age in the Hoggar, Aïr and Tibesti massifs of the Sahara, and older ones in Anatolia, Transjordan, and Aden in the Atacama desert and the Great American desert. In the neighbourhood of Death Valley, California, for instance, there are numerous small lava flows and cinder cones.

Desert conditions have occurred in various parts of the world more than once during the succession of geological ages, and have played an important role in organic evolution. The late Silurian and early Devonian periods, for instance, were characterized by increasing drought. World climates have undergone several periods of great change during the last 1000 million years. Ice ages have alternated with periods when tropical climates extended as far as 50 or 60 degrees north and south of the equator and even the polar regions were warm. In such changing conditions, places that are desert today have sometimes been well-watered while, at other times, lands now humid have been dry and barren.

Soils

The surface of desert is barren; where relief is appreciable, bare rock stands out. Soils have a restricted distribution and occur mainly on flat or

gently sloping surfaces. Elsewhere, the bare rock predominates. Weathering of the rock is largely a mechanical process, with chemical effects playing an important secondary role. Exposed rock experiences wide and rapid variations in temperature which were long thought to cause erosion by splitting and fragmentation. Serious doubt has recently been cast upon this interpretation, however, and it is now thought that moisture may play a greater part through hydration of the constituent mineral grains which results in their expansion. Moisture also supplies saline solutions to pores and cracks in rocks. When these evaporate, the salts crystallize and produce a wedging effect. The most conspicuous effect of weathering is seen in *screes*, or *bajadas*, and aprons of rock waste that, as their tops erode, gradually bury the bases of rocks, cliffs and even hills, in the products of their own decay. In time, these too disappear and the land surface may eventually become completely flat.

Rainstorms are infrequent in deserts, but when they do occur they exert a profound effect on the bare rock and soil which are not protected by vegetation. Gully and sheet erosion often occur, while watercourses are quickly choked with sand and silt. When desert *wadis* terminate in alluvial basins, the sediments they carry become stratified into layers, and gradually extend until they fill the whole internal drainage basin, forming an immense level plain. Such plains may include stony desert with a mosaic of gravel, the *reg* of the western Sahara, or of pebbles, the *serir* of Libya and Egypt. In western North America, alluvial plains are called *playas* or *sebkhas*, and temporary lakes form in them. When dry, such areas are usually covered with glistening salt. Subsurface water exerts effects that are both mechanical and also partly chemical, by transporting and depositing soluble salts.

The abrasive effects of wind erosion involve the loosening and removal of particles from the bedrock. Along with those already loosened by other processes, these are blown away. Sand is rolled along the ground, and dust and silt are carried aloft in suspension, sometimes for hundreds of miles. On settling, a thin but widespread layer of dust is formed, which may accumulate in the steppe lands bordering the desert to form the fertile *loess*. Sand travels more slowly and accumulates in dunes nearer to its source.

Rocky desert, known as *hammada* in the Sahara, is composed of weathered rock plateaux, smoothed and polished by wind abrasion. De-

Above: The Great Salt Lake of Utah is caused by evaporation in an alluvial plain or playa.

30

posited soils, composed of accumulations of medium or fine wind-blown sand, often take the form of *ergs* – vast, sandy wastes occupied by great masses of dunes. These can grow to enormous sizes, reaching heights of 200 m (656 ft) or more in the central Sahara and Rub'al Khali (or 'Empty Quarter') of Arabia, where they are known as *nefuds*.

In most deserts, dunes cover very much less than half the land surface. They are of many kinds and occur in assemblages of endless variation. There are two main types, however: crescent-shaped, moving *barchan* dunes, and *seif* or sword-shaped dunes. The latter vary in form according to the wind, to form transverse and stellar, or star-shaped dunes. Transverse dunes are created when the wind blows in a constant direction, stellar dunes in regions when it is variable.

The winnowing effect of the wind, sorting out particles of different sizes and depositing them elsewhere, results in the three main desert types: *hammada*, *reg* and *serir*, and *erg*. In semi-arid regions, where rainfall varies between about 120 and 250 mm (4½ and 10 ins) per year, the soil types usually formed are 'brown' or 'grey' semi-desert soils – the latter are sometimes called 'sierozems'. True desert soils contain no humus and are little more than fragmented rock.

Oases, whose name is derived from the Coptic words *oueh* (to dwell) and *saa* (to drink) occur in desert regions wherever water with a low concentration of salt reaches the surface – either by means of normal springs or artesian wells. They support a luxuriant vegetation and are usually densely populated. Other oases draw their waters from rivers entering the desert from nearby mountains where there is heavy rainfall or snow. Oases of this kind are found on the fringes of the Karakum desert, at Sinkiang in China, and along the foothills of the Andes. The Atacama desert, Chile, is interspersed by riverine oases, and ribbon-like oases occur along the banks of great rivers such as the Nile, Indus, Tigris, Euphrates, Colorado and Rio Grande. Altitudinal oases, such as those of the Hoggar and Tibesti mountains of the central Sahara, Jebel Marra in Darfur, Sudan, and Windhoek, in the Kalahari, depend upon local rainfall caused by their elevation. Oases with abundant water are often surrounded by salt pans (*chotts*) where the excess water collects and evaporates. The importance of oases in relation to human use of the desert is discussed in the final chapter.

The Polar Desert

Polar deserts are usually thought to be glacier-free land areas in which the mean annual rainfall is less than 25 cm (10 ins) and the mean temperature of the warmest months does not exceed 10°C (50°F). Lack of rain, however, is not a good basis for defining aridity in polar regions where evaporation is low and where water is stored inaccessibly in the form of glaciers and ice-caps. Some authorities include the glaciers themselves within the regions they designate as polar deserts. For our present purposes there seems to be no justification for excluding them. Plant growth depends very much on the presence of soil but, to an animal, it matters little whether rock, soil or ice lies beneath.

Polar regions constitute a distinct class of ecological system in which the stresses of the physical environment approach the ultimate extreme at which life is possible. For many reasons, Alpine tundras cannot so readily be regarded as deserts and, although related to the Arctic tundra, differ from it in several important features. The parallel between polar deserts and the warm deserts at lower latitudes has already been mentioned: they both have very short growth seasons and both suffer from lack of accessible moisture.

The Arctic desert

The regions around the North Pole, the northern parts of Russia, North America, Greenland and Europe are known as the Arctic desert. The North Pole itself lies beneath the Arctic ocean.

The summer has continual daylight and the winter is perpetually dark. The ocean is covered with a layer of floating ice, about 6 m (20 ft) thick, the temperature of the water being around

Left : The midnight summer sun, reflected from the polar snows, provides a little warmth to alleviate the bitter cold of the long winter night.

−2°C (28.4°F), while the temperature above is much lower. In summer, air temperatures on the land may rise above 10°C (50°F) for up to two months; there are frequent fogs and, except from the Greenland ice-cap, much of the ice and snow melts. The annual precipitation is about 25.5 cm (10 ins). Vegetation is scattered, occurring in small patches with moss, lichen, ferns and Alpine plants which produce brightly coloured flowers in summer. These are pollinated either by insects or the wind. There are some bushes but few trees. Seals, walrus, whales and many kinds of fish inhabit the sea, while on land the scanty moss and lichen support reindeer, caribou and musk-oxen. Hares, lemmings, foxes and wolves also dwell on land, while polar bears depend mainly on the sea for their food. Birds are rarely seen except in summer.

Most of the tundra occurs on the margins of Eurasia and North America, and its human inhabitants are Lapps, Samoyeds and Eskimos.

The largest tundra region is an area of 3,000,000 square kilometres (1,160,000 square miles) in northern Siberia. At most, there are 188 days in the year when the mean temperature is above freezing and, in some years, as few as 55. The low summer temperatures are due in part to the large amount of heat required to melt the ice and snow or to thaw out the ground. Near the ocean, the

winters are milder, but in the interior of the continental mass they are extremely cold. The vegetation depends upon the depth of soil that thaws in summer. Lower levels, which never melt, are known as 'permafrost'.

In the southern parts of the tundra the growing season extends from June until September, but it is even shorter nearer the North Pole. Wind is of great importance because it causes irregular drifting of the snow which, in turn, is responsible for the mosaic-like arrangement of the vegetation. In winter, wind speeds often reach 15 to 30 metres per second (30 to 70 m.p.h.). Precipitation is slight but, since potential evaporation is also very low, the climate is quite humid. Because of the permafrost, surplus water does not seep into the ground so that extensive swamps are formed. Very little peat is produced, however, because the productivity of the vegetation is so low in these areas.

The most favoured localities are south-facing stony slopes which warm up relatively well in summer because the sun is low in the sky, and consequently sometimes look like flower gardens. In contrast, flat raised ground is sparsely colonized. Not only is it warmed less by the sun, but snow is blown away so that plants are exposed to the abrasive action of ice and snow. Interminable stretches of land are covered with dwarf willow,

Left: A reindeer stag in the tundra. These domesticated animals are not migratory, and so tend to overgraze the slow-growing lichens on which they feed, unless kept on the move.

Right: Aerial view of the Arctic tundra north of Quebec. The vegetation is limited by the depth to which the soil melts in summer.

ling, or dwarf birch, while mosses predominate on wet ground and lichens on drier soils.

The first impression of the tundra in summer is one of utter desolation. The rivers are flanked by swamps, or strewn with blocks of ice and littered with bleached, shattered timber brought down from the taiga forest zone by the floods. The landscape is immense and bleak, apparently without grace or dignity of any kind. A natural wasteland, it may, at first sight, appear quite repellent. Yet, for some, it has a marked attraction like the fascination, for others, of the sandy desert regions of warmer climes. The contours of the country acquire a new importance, and the bare, simple, landscape takes on a romance and beauty that are quite at variance with the dreary impression first created.

Antarctica

Unlike the northern polar regions, there are no trees and very few plants on the Antarctic continent although it is equivalent in size to Australia and Europe without Russia. The elevated interior of the continent is covered by vast glaciers, but its margins are low-lying. Western Antarctica consists of folded ranges and plateaux while the centre of the continent is divided into two regions

Above: Even in the summer, most of the Antarctic continent is covered with glaciers – seen here by the light of the midnight sun.

Left: Alpine and Arctic plants are squat and low-growing, but they are mostly pollinated by insects and consequently bear brightly coloured blossoms.

separated by a zone of subsidence extending from the Ross to the Weddell Seas.

The continental glacier is more than 1800 m (6000 ft) thick in places, decreasing to about one-sixth of this near the coast. Its greatest elevation is about 3300 m (11,000 ft) near the South Pole. The land is surrounded by floating shelf-ice, beyond which sea-ice extends for varying distances, depending on the season. Plants and animals are very poorly represented.

The vegetation of polar deserts

The plants of the polar desert environment are small, close to the ground and widely separated, with bare rock or soil between them. They are anchored against the wind by deep top roots or take the form of flexible cushions of intertwined strands. There is little modification of the micro-climate by the vegetation except in so far as it engenders the accumulation of snowdrifts. Like Alpine species, the plants of Arctic regions are specially adapted to metabolizing, growing and reproducing at low temperatures. They are almost exclusively perennial and take the form of low bushes, recumbent or mat-like in habit. Herbs generally have a cushion-like form, or a basal rosette with large roots, rhizomes or bulb-storage organs. Their leaves frequently have leathery, waxy or hairy surfaces which serve to reduce

water-loss by evaporation. Lichens and mosses comprise an important element of the flora.

Seeds remain dormant for long periods of time when the temperature is low, because they require temperatures well above freezing for germination to take place. Consequently, the establishment of seedlings is a rare and slow process, often requiring several years for its completion. Seed production is opportunist, and vegetative reproduction by rhizomes, bulbils or layering is common. (Rhizomes are underground stems bearing buds in the axils of reduced, scale-like leaves.) Pollination is mostly by insects – flies are more important than bees in this respect – but wind pollination becomes of greater importance in the highest latitudes. Buds are preformed the year before flowering because there is not sufficient time for both bud-formation and flowering in a single season.

Arctic plants do not appear to possess much intrinsic dormancy, but seeds retain their viability for long periods, and there is some evidence that both seeds and lichens from Arctic areas may be able to remain alive for several thousands of years in soil that is permanently frozen. The development of many plants is protracted and can be broken off at any stage for the winter. In this way, they are little affected by the shortness of the summer and may flower during any stage of the

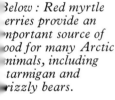

Below : Red myrtle berries provide an important source of food for many Arctic animals, including ptarmigan and grizzly bears.

vegetational season, the buds having been formed one, or even two, years previously. Most seeds and fruits are dispersed by the wind which blows them across the snow so that they land up in accumulations in hollows, slopes and other favoured localities. A few are dispersed by water. Seeds are almost invariably very small, and germinate extremely rapidly in the spring. The seeds of some grasses even germinate before they have left the parent plant. Flowering plants sometimes produce berries that are fed on by a variety of birds and mammals, including the Alaskan grizzly bear.

The animals of polar deserts

Arctic polar desert animals can be grouped into the following categories: large carnivores active throughout the year, such as the polar bear and wolf; small carnivores, such as the fox and weasel, which are also in evidence the whole year; large migrant herbivores, such as the caribou and musk-ox; small herbivores which may be abundant locally – these include lemming and arctic hare; resident birds, including ptarmigan and snowy owl; migrant birds – geese, ducks and passerines or perching birds; flying insects; and soil invertebrates – spring-tails, mite, water-

bears and nematode worms. In Antarctica, only the soil invertebrate and migrant bird categories are represented.

Because the vegetation is negligible, the fauna is correspondingly scarce. Indeed, the vertebrate fauna of the Antarctic continent is confined to birds and mammals that, directly or indirectly, depend on the sea for their food. These birds include penguins and the skuas that prey on their young, while the mammals are represented by seals and sea-elephants. Apart from parasites, the invertebrate fauna is restricted to spring-tails, mites, water-bears, rotifers or wheel-animalcules and a wingless midge that inhabits penguin rookeries. These are active only for a short period each year and exist for the rest of the year in a frozen state.

Environmental temperatures have a considerable influence on the sizes and dimensions of animals. The fishes that live in cold waters tend to be larger and to have more vertebrae than their relatives from warmer seas. This observation was first made by David Starr Jordan, a nineteenth century American zoologist. The proportions of the body are also an important factor in temperature regulation, especially among terrestrial animals. The effect of climate on the evolution of

Above: Polar bears in the Arctic desert survive mainly on fish and seals.

38

the proportions of the limbs of animals was noted by J. A. Allen of the American Museum of Natural History, also in the last century. It is known that the radiation potential of a cylinder increases in proportion to the square of its diameter. This simple fact is probably responsible to a great extent for the lean and lanky build of most of the larger vertebrates, such as goats, camels and gazelles, that inhabit hot desert and semi-arid regions of the world. Conversely, the mammals from the Arctic tend to have short legs and stocky bodies. The musk-ox, for example, stands only one metre (over three feet) high, although it is two and a half metres in length (eight feet). Its neck is fairly thick, its tail very short and its ears are hidden in its furry coat.

Carl Bergman's rule, first formulated in 1847, states that warm-blooded mammals and birds from colder climates are larger, and therefore have proportionately less surface area from which to lose heat, than corresponding homeotherms of warmer regions. Although the African elephant is an apparent exception, its surface area is increased approximately one-third by its enormous ears. These have a rich blood supply and, almost certainly, serve as radiators for cooling the body during the heat of the day. The significance

of this becomes even more obvious when one remembers that an elephant may weigh as much as one million mice, but its linear dimensions are only one hundred times greater.

The physiological implications of size are considerable. They affect all aspects of an animal's life, from its embryological development and growth to the amount and nature of the food that it requires. The relative dimensions of the different organs of the body of an animal also depend upon its size. Indeed, size is perhaps the most important single factor influencing physiological processes, as well as morphological relationships, in terrestrial animals.

In contrast to the Antarctic, Arctic regions have a comparatively richer fauna that is independent of the sea but, of course, the number of species and individuals decreases towards the Pole. Every polar desert soil that thaws for some part of the year appears to contain nematode worms and water-bears. These probably feed upon humus and moulds that inhabit the soil. A remarkable fauna of earthworms, insects and arachnids also inhabits regions of snow and ice. Their dark colours enable them to absorb the scanty warmth of the sun's heat upon which their metabolism depends. Dead insects, blown on to

Above: Crane-flies or daddy-long-legs are characteristic Arctic insects. The insects shown here (male on the right) are mating on a log of wood. The larvae are soil dwellers.

Top right: Sandy desert fox found in North American deserts. These foxes frequent the plains from Mexico to Saskatchewan.

Bottom right: Rockhopper penguins breed in New Zealand, Tristan da Cunha, Gough Island, the Falkland Islands and various islands of the Antarctic. Penguins are long-lived, monogamous birds, often maintaining the pair-bond for life.

glaciers, are often to be seen in depressions where the warmth they have absorbed from the sun has melted for each of them an icy grave.

Earthworms are often found frozen in ice, and one species can even bore through hard-packed snow, feeding on minute soil algae – but probably part of its life-history is spent in the soil.

The land and freshwater snails of the Arctic are small and occur principally on the borders of springs. They are an unimportant element of the fauna. Several insects are found, of which flies predominate. These are followed in numbers by saw-flies, and bumble-bees, springtails and moths. The composition of the fauna depends both upon available food and upon resistance to cold. Insects that feed on green plants do not penetrate so far to the north as do species that feed on lichen, plant remains or animal food. It seems likely that spring-tails form a basis of food-chains in regions of snow and ice, just as bristle-tails do in hot and temperate deserts. One of them, the so-called 'snow-flea' of Spitzbergen, forms great black masses, sometimes extending over an area of about 900 square centimetres (one square foot) or more. Mosquitoes, black-flies and other biting flies form a veritable plague during the short Arctic summer. They have in common

the possession of an aquatic larval stage. The commonest ground-living animals of the Arctic are undoubtedly wolf-spiders and, in Iceland, harvest-spiders too.

Beyond the northern limits of the coniferous forest there are no wasps except a few ichneumons. The only bees are bumble-bees, but day-flying butterflies and moths may sometimes be very numerous (except in Iceland where these insects are poorly represented). Tundra beetles belong chiefly to families that are carnivorous or feed on carrion – vegetable feeders, such as weevils, are scarce. The dominant insects are flies – especially biting flies with aquatic larvae, including mosquitoes, midges and black-flies. In addition to these pests, caribou are tormented by nostril flies and warble flies. The larvae of the former parasitize the caribou's nasal passages and sinuses, while those of the latter form swellings beneath the skin of the back.

The composition of the Arctic insect fauna is very different from that of temperate regions, and the number of species very much lower. In the low Arctic the number may be reduced to about five per cent and, on Queen Elizabeth Island, it is only about one per cent of the number found in comparable temperate areas. Many of the endemic forms are adapted to special features of the environment, especially the low temperature and short season.

The Arctic environment is not inherently simple, nor does it forbid a greater diversity. It seems to lie beyond the range of physiological tolerance of all but a very few of the forms of temperate origin. The greatest continuity of evolutionary history has occurred in the tropics, to which are adapted most forms of life. Given time, however, there is no apparent reason why a greater diversity of Arctic forms should not eventually develop – unless, of course, the climate changes again and a new ice age destroys them all.

Amphibians and reptiles cannot live in really cold regions, but the adder occurs in Europe as far north as the Arctic Circle and the garter snake has been recorded in Alaska. These animals hibernate in deep burrows during the winter and are live-bearing species. Reptile eggs could not develop on account of low air temperatures and the shortness of the summer but, by basking in any available warmth, viviparous snakes are able to speed the embryological development of their young enough for them to be born before the end of the summer.

Apart from thick fur and insulating fat, the mammals of the Arctic have little special protection against the winter's cold, nor can they migrate to warmer places like birds do. As we

have seen, however, extremities such as legs and ears, from which heat is lost, tend to be short and rounded. Moreover, the feet of penguins, gulls and other birds function at very low temperatures. A heat-exchange system of entwined veins and arteries cools the blood flowing to the extremities so that warmth is not wasted. The system can serve two purposes – circulation is restricted and heat retained when the surroundings are cold yet blood can be flushed to the extremities if the animal needs to lose heat. The most striking species are the polar bear, caribou, lemming, Arctic fox, Arctic hare, wolf and stoat. The Siberian tundra also possesses a few species which are really forest forms, like the glutton or wolverine, the brown bear, common fox, and some voles.

In summer the wild reindeer range up to the shores of the Arctic Ocean, frequenting chiefly the high ground which is comparatively free from mosquitoes. The fawns are dropped in May and the Samoyeds of the Yenisei, USSR, say that at this time there is a 'Truce of God' between the deer and their enemies, the wolves. Both species resort to the same parts of the tundra to breed and, for a short time, live there in harmony. The explanation, however, is not that wolves have sentimental scruples but that, in summer, lemmings afford them abundant alternative food.

twice as long as those of an ordinary rabbit. Ungulates are sometimes unable to cross snow surfaces that will bear the weight of lighter predators such as wolves, lynxes and bob-cats. They counter this hazard, however, by making trails and ranges where the snow is trampled hard: Canadian moose may sometimes be restricted to an area of less than a 100 m (328 ft) radius. Ungulates frequently paw the snow to reach the underlying vegetation, and are often accompanied by ptarmigan which are thereby also enabled to feed.

The characteristic marine mammals of the Poles, the walruses and seals, spend a considerable part of their lives on shore, especially during the breeding season. Some species of seal migrate to temperate regions in winter and thus avoid the intense cold, but others live permanently in the coldest regions and make breathing holes through the ice.

Birds are the most conspicuous animals of the tundra in summer, but only the hardiest are able to winter in the north. Despite the tremendous distances they have to fly, most species arrive at the beginning of summer in a fat and healthy state. At first there is little food available for them, and all their activities appear to be concentrated on establishing territories, courtship and mating. Later, as the thaw sets in, mosquitoes appear in

Above: Caribou migrating. In parts of Newfoundland, vast herds have, over the years, worn away the rocks to a depth of half a metre or more (about two feet).

Left: The grizzly bear, the largest carnivore of North America, is found in the western half of the continent from the Arctic Ocean to northern Mexico, but is most common in British Columbia, the Yukon and Alaska.

Right: The elk, largest of European deers, is found chiefly in an area extending eastwards from Scandinavia, Finland and northern Russia to Siberia. It is almost identical with the American moose of the northern United States and Canada.

Musk-oxen, which are more closely related to sheep and goats than to cattle, protect their young from wolves by forming a defensive circle around them. The same formation is also adopted to shield the calves from blizzards.

Caribou are migratory and so do not overgraze the slow-growing lichens on which they feed, although they may move in enormous herds. In parts of Newfoundland, the rocks are worn away to a depth of half a metre by the many thousands of hooves that have passed over them for countless years of migration. When domesticated reindeer were introduced into Alaska at the end of the last century their numbers increased to over half a million and then declined catastrophically. Their relatively sedentary habits had led to destruction of the food supplies essential for survival in winter. Complete recovery of the lichen requires at least 25 years, and its ecology is complicated.

Many Arctic mammals and birds have evolved relatively large feet which act as snow-shoes. The spreading hooves of the caribou, in the same way as the polar bear's furry feet, give purchase against firm snow. Ptarmigan and grouse have feathered feet with widened toes, while the pads of the hind legs of the snowshoe rabbit are almost

great numbers and their larvae are devoured not only by small waders and passerine birds, but by larger forms such as gulls, ducks and sandpipers. Most Arctic birds have a wide range of diet, stints and plovers even eating willow buds and golden plovers swallowing crowberries.

One of the reasons why some species of plovers, in particular, are able to inhabit the frozen north is that, as in snipes too, both parents help to rear the brood. Moreover, not only do the young develop extremely rapidly after hatching, thus shortening the period of dependence on their parents, but social tendencies are strongly marked, providing the protection of numbers. Arctic terns breed in colonies and will drive off enemies many times larger than themselves, diving at them and then swooping up to renew the attack.

In temperate climates, most birds begin to moult their summer dress as soon as their young are fledged. In the Arctic summer this process must be accelerated if the new plumage is to be ready for the autumn migration. Feathers are sometimes shed so rapidly that, for a while, the birds are almost incapable of flight. In the far north, the ptarmigan moults three times between June and September – from winter to summer plumage, from summer to autumn and back to winter white again. This species does not migrate, but digs tunnels in the snow where it finds shelter and food.

Green plants, especially grass and Arctic willow, form the staple food of geese, grouse and lemmings. Other animals rely on them to a lesser extent. Reindeer graze on them, and they provide cover for nesting birds. Lemmings comprise the main food item of foxes, wolves and birds of prey. Passerine or perching birds, and waders, feed mainly on mosquitoes, their larvae and other small aquatic animals.

Activity rhythms and cycles of animals During the summer season, the moist Arctic soil teems with invertebrate animals. Most tundra insects, however, require two summer seasons to complete their development. Fly larvae swarm in every summer pool and are fed on by birds and fishes. Migrant passerine birds come into the tundra in vast numbers to nest, as do waterfowl where lakes and marshes afford them feeding grounds.

Small herbivores, especially lemmings, may be abundant in the more thickly vegetated regions of the tundra where numbers of herbaceous plants are found. In the less productive regions, caribou and musk-oxen graze, especially on lichens.

Animals that live in Arctic regions must be able to survive the change from the cold and darkness of winter to the warmth and light of summer and

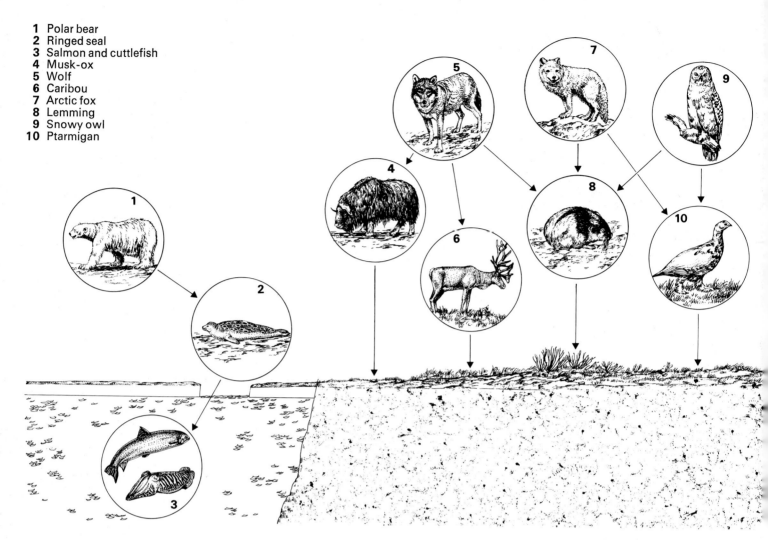

1 Polar bear
2 Ringed seal
3 Salmon and cuttlefish
4 Musk-ox
5 Wolf
6 Caribou
7 Arctic fox
8 Lemming
9 Snowy owl
10 Ptarmigan

vice versa. Some of them pass the winter shelter-ing underground; others remain in the open, taking cover only during the worst storms.

During the winter, the ground is covered with a deep layer of snow. This provides cover or insulation for the animals, such as lemmings, that live beneath it. These neither store food in summer nor do they hibernate. In winter they dig long tunnels in the snow, just above the ground, from which they search for plants and especially grass roots. They still keep their burrows in the earth, but cannot enlarge these until the summer, because the soil is completely frozen.

Arctic hares live above ground and continue feeding throughout the winter, usually in places where the snow has blown away and left the plants exposed. The Arctic fox likewise feeds through-out the winter, but has difficulty in finding enough to eat. It begins to store food – birds, eggs, lemmings and so on – before the winter begins, hiding it in a cache underneath rocks, or covering it with gravel.

Most species produce their young at the beginning of the summer when the weather is warmer and food plentiful. The female musk-ox bears a single calf at the end of April which can walk an hour after birth, but she feeds it for a year

or more. Not many birds remain in the Arctic during the winter. Ptarmigan and snowy owls are exceptional in this respect. Ptarmigan feed on moss and lichen, and berries when these are available. Insects form a large part of the diet of the chicks. Snowy owls are predators on lem-mings and other small mammals, water-fowl and even fish, though their heavily muffled feet seem most unsuited for fishing. This large species of owl hunts both by day and by night. As soon as the spring begins, migratory birds arrive in their hundreds of thousands to feed and breed in the continuous daylight of the Arctic summer. Many of them are sea-birds and waterfowl that find breeding places on cliffs and on the islands which fringe the coastline.

Resident mammals of the polar deserts give birth when conditions are most favourable for the survival of the young. This is sometimes achieved by 'delayed implantation' – the egg does not become attached to the wall of the womb until environmental conditions favour development. Although 'delayed implantation' is by no means restricted to Arctic and Antarctic species, it is particularly common in high latitudes.

Several species of bird do not breed when food supplies fail or when weather conditions are

Above: A typical food-chain in the Arctic, which shows carnivores feeding on herbivores; the main food of the polar bear, however, is the seal, itself a carnivore feeding on fish.

Right: The snowy owl is a formidable predator on ptarmigans, lemmings and other animals of the Arctic, hunting both by day and by night.

unsatisfactory at the start of the season. These include the eider duck and snowy owl.

Few animal populations remain constant in size for very long. In addition to seasonal cycles in numbers, cyclic variation in numbers over periods of several years is seen especially among the mammals and birds of the Arctic and cool temperate regions of the world. Two or three main cycles seem to occur. First, there is a three-year or four-year cycle in the numbers of various mammals whose food is based on the lemmings. This is seen, for example, in the white or Arctic fox, and in the snowy owl which although it does not normally migrate, may be forced by starvation to fly hundreds of miles to the south. Secondly, there is a four-year cycle in the animals of the belt of open forest lying between the tundra and the taiga. This is based on voles. Thirdly, there is a ten-year cycle in populations of the snowshoe rabbit and other animals of the northern forest regions of North America.

It has been suggested that the dominant rodent interacts with its vegetable food to produce a predator-prey oscillation. When the numbers of rodents decline, predatory forms themselves also decrease, thereby allowing an increase in gallinaceous birds such as ptarmigans. The regularity

of the cycles may be because the basic predator-prey oscillations are less disturbed by other factors than in more complex environments. The phenomenon is, however, little understood.

Cyclic fluctuations in numbers have two main advantages to a species; they permit numbers to be adjusted to variations in environmental conditions, and they allow evolutionary change to be more rapid than it would be in a species with constant numbers. This is because, while the numbers of a population are increasing, selection is weak since a larger proportion of individuals are able to survive than when numbers are constant: consequently, the population becomes more than normally variable. When it reaches its maximum, however, this variable population is subjected to natural selection. Any variations that happen to be advantageous are then selected. Thus a biological advantage accrues to species whose numbers tend to fluctuate cyclically, in addition to any incidental increase in distribution caused by emigration.

Fluctuations in populations of lemmings and other small herbivores are passed on to their predators such as foxes, snowy owls and other carnivorous birds, so that the whole system is jolted. Some of the grasses which grow in stand-ing water thrive best when regularly grazed by lemmings because this prevents old, dead leaves from burying the rhizomes in humus from which nutrients are not readily released. Consequently, plants, as well as animals, show fluctuations in their numbers.

Migration Whereas the majority of insects pass the winter in a resting stage and birds migrate to warmer climes, Arctic mammals do neither. Hibernation does not take place – probably because the short, cold summer does not allow sufficient accumulation of the necessary food reserves. Also, the large amount of snow partly removes the need for hibernation because it provides an insulating layer below which small animals can burrow. At the same time it enables them to browse on leaves and twigs that would otherwise lie beyond their reach.

It is true that deer move southwards towards the forest and wolves follow them, but this provides but a slight amelioration of the cruel conditions in which they have to survive. In any case, smaller forms such as lemmings remain in their summer haunts, feeding on herbage buried under the snow. They are incapable of travelling far enough to reach a warmer climate.

Lemmings from Greenland, however, move

over the frozen ocean to the mainland from islands 50 km (30 miles) distant. When the ice breaks, the little creatures run backwards and forwards along the banks of streams and rivers, looking for a smooth place with a slow current at which to cross. Having found one, they at once jump in and swim rapidly to the other side where they give themselves a good shake as a dog would, and then continue their journey as if nothing had happened.

Lemmings wander erratically and no definite path is chosen, but the general direction is determined partly by the nature of the ground traversed. Water is no obstacle, but the legend of self-destruction may have arisen out of incidents such as when, in 1868, a steamer in Trondheim Fiord sailed for 15 minutes through a pack of swimming lemmings. Migrating hares and rabbits are also known to swim rivers and, in 1867, a swarm of squirrels is reported to have invaded Tapilah in the Urals, USSR, swimming the Tchossoveia River and climbing up the oars of boats which crossed their track. Lemmings can swim across fiords more than two and a half kilometres (one and a half miles) in width. It is therefore not surprising that they should sometimes be swept away by the tide.

Animal coloration The dark colours of the insects that inhabit lands of snow and ice may help in the absorption of warmth from the sun. The white coloration of Arctic mammals and birds, on the other hand, has sometimes been ascribed to the effects of cold. Yet several forms, like the sable, glutton (wolverine) and raven, which are influenced by this very factor to which whiteness has been ascribed, remain brown or black throughout the year. The explanation of this inconsistency is readily apparent as we shall see. Furthermore, seasonal colour change is an hereditary factor, under genetic control; Arctic foxes, for example, living in zoological gardens, where they experience temperate climatic conditions, still regularly become white each autumn. The sable and glutton have no special need for concealment. The former lives and hunts its prey among fir trees where its rich brown coat harmonizes with the bark, while the glutton is exclusively nocturnal and partly a carrion feeder with few potential enemies.

In Arctic regions the raven, an omnivorous scavenger, with no potential enemies to fear, retains its black coat throughout the year. In contrast, the snowy owl, a predator to whom it is undoubtedly useful to be inconspicuous when hunting by daylight during the long Arctic summer, is white throughout the year. Cryptic or concealing coloration is beneficial to most predators because it enables them to stalk their prey unobserved. It is found in the polar bear, Arctic fox and ermine. In summer, when the snow melts, the Arctic fox and ermine lose their white coats and acquire brown hairs which allow them to remain inconspicuous against the background of exposed rock and soil.

The same is true of different herbivorous animals: the ptarmigan becomes white in winter, but moults in the spring so that it matches its background. Even when ptarmigan are actually moulting, so that only some of their feathers are white, they still remain inconspicuous among the spring and autumn snow patches. White winter coats provide the inconspicuousness that is the chief means of protection to snowshoe rabbits and willow grouse. Even in the north of Scotland the stoat, weasel, and mountain hare become white in

Above : The ermine is a stoat whose winter dress is entirely white, save for the black tip of the tail. These voracious animals feed on small mammals, birds and their eggs.

Right : The Arctic fox is dark brown or slate-coloured in summer, but white in winter.

winter. The pine martin, which does not change colour, is chiefly arboreal (tree-dwelling) and, in the trees, would be conspicuous if white; snow-shoe rabbits, which shelter in burrows, also do not acquire white coats in winter.

Man and the polar desert

The polar regions are among the last of the earth's terrestrial biomes to be explored and investigated. Their rigorous climate and geographical isolation has made them so unattractive for human occupation that only a few groups of Eskimos inhabit the Arctic permanently, and the Antarctic has no indigenous population at all. The recent discovery of oil and other resources, however, has prompted an influx of people and machinery whose impact on the Arctic environment is con-

siderable. Disturbance has been caused by con struction works, transportation, exploration, an activities related to water supply and waste dis posal. The use of snowmobiles by Eskimo hunter and trappers has increased their efficiency to suc an extent that the wildlife is being over-exploited The vegetation is being damaged by ski trails, an through constant overgrazing by domestic musk oxen and reindeer. The tundra is a simpl ecosystem, easily destroyed by misuse.

The indigenous peoples of the Arctic have stake in the economic development of their land that deserves recognition, even though it is ofte ignored or overlooked. They depend completel on the natural fauna for their livelihood. Fo centuries they have harvested the wildlife an other renewable resources of the country, carin

little for the mineral wealth that lay underground because it had no value in their economy. Their numbers remained low as a result of starvation, disease and a high infantile mortality rate, and their activities had little environmental impact. Not until man and machines from the more complex world to the south appeared to extract oil and mine ores, did the native populations become aware of the importance of their land to others. With improved medical facilities and hygiene, their numbers have increased, as have their material desires. Human history has continually been scarred by similar clashes between the cultures of ancient peoples and that of western technology. Economic development of the Arctic regions will undoubtedly leave scars not only on the land but also on its people.

The World's Major Deserts

The chief low latitude deserts of the world, summarized in the table at the end of this chapter, are as follows:

The Sahara

Named from the Arabic word meaning 'desert' or 'wilderness', the world's largest desert stretches across Africa from the Atlantic through Egypt to the Red Sea and includes the Somali desert to the south-east. As part of the Great Palaearctic desert, it continues through Arabia and Iran into northern India and central Asia. On the north, the Sahara is bounded by the Mediterranean and on the south by the arid Sahel savanna region of tropical Africa. The Saharan platform, upon which later deposits have been laid, consists of the oldest sedimentary rocks, of Archaean or Pre-Cambrian age, which have been much folded and denuded. Vertical movements and erosion have resulted in the formation of deep valleys and gorges, such as those of the Tassili mountains.

Most of the land surface is now occupied by *erg*, *reg* or *hammada*. *Erg* is the desert of shifting sand dunes, such as that in Algeria between Béni-Abbès and Ghadames and in much of the Libyan desert. The *reg* desert consists of wind-scoured plains strewn with gravel and boulders, while the hammada are rocky plateaux with bare rock outcrops and deeply eroded gorges, found chiefly around the mountains of Hoggar in Algeria and Tibesti in Chad. The Sahara is one of the hottest regions of the world, with mean annual temperatures exceeding 30°C (85°F). The hottest months are June, July and August and shade temperatures of 58°C (136.5°F) have been recorded. There is a tendency for rain to fall in sudden storms at irregular intervals, but the desert as a whole is characterized by drought. The southern fringe receives rain in summer.

The vegetation of most of the Sahara is poorly developed, but regions from which plant life is entirely absent are scarce. Examples of completely barren desert can be found in the Algerian Tanezrouft, in the *hammada* of Tinghert, south of Ghadames in Libya, and in the Libyan and Nubian desert regions. In general, the vegetation consists either of permanent trees and shrubs, such as acacia, betoum, tamarisks and jujubes, and delicate ephemerals which provide fodder for camels, goats and nomadic game animals. This ephemeral vegetation is known to the inhabitants of the Sahara as *acheb*. The natural vegetation of the oases was oleander and tamarisks: date palms have subsequently been introduced. The fauna includes gazelles, oryx, addax and other antelopes, jackals, foxes and badgers. Lions were exterminated during the last century. The first inhabitants were probably Negroes who retreated in the face of the advancing Berbers, themselves afterwards pushed back by the Arabs. From a mixture of these emerged the three great ethnic groups of today: the Tuareg, Tibbu and Moors.

The Arabian, Iranian and Turkestan deserts

These are eastward extensions of the Sahara and form a continuation of the Great Palaearctic desert. From a sandy coasted plain which borders the Red Sea, a high mountain chain rises abruptly to 2400 m (8000 ft), behind which lies the extensive plateau of the Nejd. The Turkestan and Iranian deserts of western and central Asia consist of other extensive plateaux crossed by arid mountain ranges. Climatic conditions are variable, a general aridity being combined with

Left: Dunes of the Algerian sand sea. Wind-carried sand grains are rounded so that they move easily. Following pages: Mountains, wadi, and saline deposits in the Band-i-Amir region of Afghanistan.

extremes of heat and cold, which are even greater further east in the Takla-Makan (China) and Gobi (Mongolia) deserts.

The southern portion of the Arabian desert is much like the Sahara, and its flora and fauna are similar. There are sand dunes, especially in the coastal regions, and a cover of desert soils inland, overlying a basement of crystalline rocks that reaches an altitude of more than 2800 m (9300 ft) in the western highlands. The Turkestan desert, USSR, includes extensive dunes, alluvial plains, depressions, river terraces and flood plains. The black sands of the Karakum and the red sands of the Kyzyl-Kum regions in the USSR are interspersed with saline soils. Gravel is confined to the foothills of the mountains on the south and east, and the plateaux in the north-west.

The human inhabitants of the Arabian desert include nomadic Bedouin tribes. On the Oman coast there are also a number of Negroes.

The Takla-Makan and Gobi deserts

These represent the extreme eastern extensions of the Great Palaearctic desert into Mongolia and western China. They experience hot summers and very cold winters. The central portion of the Takla-Makan consists of a wide expanse of shift-ing sands that have been moving southward for centuries. Some of the dunes are said to be over 90 m (300 ft) high, although most of them are about one-tenth of this size. Several rivers flow into the desert from the Tien Shan (Sinkiang) and Kunlun Shan (China), the mountain ranges surrounding it. The Gobi extends from the foot of the Pamirs eastwards to the Great Kingan mountains, and from the Altai, Khangai and Yablonoi mountains in the north to the Altyn Tagh and Nan Shan in the south. Gobi itself occupies a broad, shallow depression in the wide plateau separating the northern ranges of Tibet and the Altai at an average altitude of 900 m (3000 ft) in the east and of about 1500 m (5000 ft) in the south and west. The relief features are the result of warping and uplift, and there is an alternating succession of broad, gravel plains with isolated hills and low flat-topped ranges. Dry river beds and the signs of old lakes provide clear evidence of climatic changes in the remote past.

Trees are almost unknown in the Gobi – only willow, poplar, elm and birch are found – and there are no oases to relieve the unbroken stretches of sand, gravel or saline clay. Water is found only at wells or in occasional small alkaline lakes. The vegetation consists of grass, thorn and patches of

Above: Beisa oryx found in arid regions from Tanzania to Ethiopia and the Red Sea hills of the Sudan.

Above: A scene in the Gobi desert of Outer Mongolia. This is a desert in which the winters are cold but the summers are hot.

scrub. Several kinds of bush pea with yellow or pink flowers, salt bush, camel sage and plains onion are the most abundant plants in Mongolia.

The commonest animal in the Pamirs, Mongolia, is the yak, which is not only wild but domesticated on a large scale. Other creatures of the mountains and desert include gazelles, Marco Polo sheep or argali, and the rare Mongolian wild horse. The most characteristic and abundant animal of the true Gobi is the long-tailed gazelle. These gazelles are found singly, in pairs or in herds of up to ten or twelve, but they do not gather together in great herds during spring and autumn as do the gazelles of the neighbouring grassland, presumably because the vegetation is too sparse to provide enough food to support a large group. Small mammals include the pale coloured and three-toed jerboa, desert hamster, hedgehog, shrew and sand rat. There is an abundant bird fauna which, of course, is not confined to the desert areas. This includes sand grouse, great bustard, demoiselle crane, and a variety of eagles, hawks and vultures. The many salt and brackish lakes are the home of ducks and other waterfowl. Reptiles are scarce because the cold winters are unfavourable to cold-blooded animals.

The Thar desert

The Indian or Thar desert is a south-eastern extension of the Iranian desert, and forms the last part of the Great Palaearctic desert region. It lies between the ancient Aravalli mountains and the steep, folded ranges west of the Indus, and extends from the shores of the Arabian sea almost to the Himalayas, thus including much of Pakistan as well as eastern India. Although there is considerable topographic and climatic diversity, the Thar desert is a major natural entity, which may be described as 'arid lowland'. It is covered with a deep mantle of alluvial and wind-borne deposits, and is characterized by daily and seasonal climatic extremes, with a hot season from March to October. Minimum temperatures occur in January. The moist air flow of the summer monsoon passes nearby, to the east, and this provides the rain that falls in July and August.

The entire desert consists of level or gently sloping plains broken up by dunes and low barren plains. The vegetation varies according to whether the plant communities are adapted to salt desert, clay desert, *hammada* or *erg*. It is varied and open, with shrubs and coarse herbaceous plants, salt-loving species being conspicuous. The fauna includes camels, cattle, sheep, goats, and a

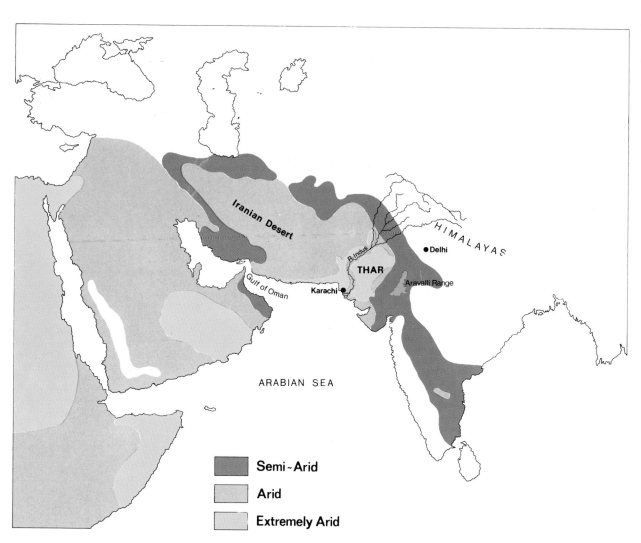

Semi-Arid

Arid

Extremely Arid

variety of wild animals including wild asses, hyaenas, jackals, foxes, hares and rabbits.

The Kalahari and Namib deserts

The Kalahari forms part of the immense inner tableland of southern Africa. Its northern section joins the Namib desert to the west but, southwards, the two deserts are separated by the Nama and Namara hills. The northern edge of the Kalahari coincides with the valley of the Okavango River and the bed of Lake Ngami, the southern with the Orange River. Eastward, the desert grades into cultivated land. The average elevation is 900 to 1220 m (3000 to 4000 ft) and there is a gentle slope from east to west with a dip to the north.

Most of the Kalahari consists of red sand which forms long shifting dunes with sparse grass cover, especially in the eastern region. There are also very extensive dunes in the Namib. The sand dunes of Algoa Bay, east of Port Elizabeth, South Africa, reach considerable heights, and extend far inland so that they present the appearance of a sea of sand, reminiscent of the *ergs* of the Sahara.

Although remarkably flat, the Kalahari desert is intersected by the beds of ancient rivers with extensive mud flats and deposits of alluvium.

After rain, these form pans or lakes which retain water for several months and are much frequented by game animals. The northern half of the Namib desert consists of gravel plains, occasionally interrupted by *inselbergs* – isolated hills with steep slopes characteristic of tropical regions.

The Kalahari is called a desert because there is little permanent surface water, but its vegetation is actually quite rich. The north and west are covered with dense scrub and scattered thorn trees interspersed with tall palms. Watermelons and plants with large tubers are characteristic. The fauna is likewise rich, and many species of big game are found including gemsbok. The human inhabitants are bushmen and Hottentots.

The cold Benguéla current which sweeps up the western coast of southern Africa is indirectly responsible for the extreme aridity of the Namib whose annual rainfall averages only 23 mm (0.9 ins). The prevailing winds are the cool, south-westerly sea breeze and the desiccating easterly 'berg' wind which are together responsible for sculpturing the large parallel sand dunes of the southern Namib. The sea breeze produces fog throughout the year which is responsible for 33 mm (1.3 ins) precipitation at Gobabeb. Upon this depends much of the fauna and flora of the

area, including the rare welwitschia plant which may live for 1500 to 2000 years. The annual temperature range is only 6.5°C (44°F) per year, and frost is almost unknown. The average daily range is 16 to 18.5°C (61° to 65°F), but extreme daytime temperatures of 40°C (104°F) are occasionally associated with 'berg' winds.

The Australian desert

Most of central Australia, about three-quarters of the entire continent, is occupied by desert and semi-desert. The western plateau with an altitude of 150 to 600 m (500 to 2000 ft), is mainly semi-desert, which gives way to desert conditions in the heart of the continent. The Simpson desert, north of Lake Eyre, lies below 150 m (500 ft). Coastal deserts are found in the southern and western parts of the continent where conditions are much less extreme than in the Sahara.

The vegetation of the Australian desert is rich. It is dominated by dwarf eucalyptus scrub, known as *mallee*, or by acacia scrub or *mulga*. The latter covers an extensive zone in the Eremean province of Western Australia, reaching to the coastal zone south of the Hamersley ranges. It forms an almost continuous belt across the centre of South Australia into north-western New South Wales and south-west Queensland, where it is strongly developed. Fringing the deserts are arid formations with perennial grass in the northern area with summer rainfall and succulent shrubs prominent in the south where rain falls in the winter. As a result of the aridity of the climate, bush fires are frequent and the seeds of many plants are not only resistant to fire but seldom germinate truly unless fire has passed over them.

The comparative paucity of the vertebrate fauna is a striking characteristic of the entire Australian region. Biologically, however, the fauna is an extremely interesting one. The dominant mammals are marsupials which have evolved and radiated into the various ecological niches occupied in other realms by placental mammals. Marsupials give birth to their young while these are in a very undeveloped state, but the females carry their babies in a pouch or marsupium until they are old enough to fend for themselves. The chief members of the order are the kangaroos and wallabies, the wombat and the Tasmanian wolf – the latter being almost extinct. The avian fauna includes the flightless emu, parrots, quail, birds of prey, and many perching birds. The reptilian fauna is likewise variable, containing many lizards and snakes.

Before the coming of white man, the Australian desert was inhabited only by aborigines who survived through a detailed knowledge of the habits, cycles, food plants and animals of the area.

The Great American desert

The deserts of North America extend from the south-western regions of the United States southwards into Baja California and the mainland of Mexico where they occupy the lowlands of Sonora as far south as the delta of the Yaqui river in Mexico. Because of the great variations of climate, physiography and geography, there is a great diversity of soils. Sand dunes and hummocks are generally smaller than those of the Great Palaearctic desert. The scenery is affected more by the presence of the mountains than by any other geological feature. Their bare rocky flanks are slashed by innumerable intricately branched gulleys, tortuous valleys and boulder-strewn canyons from whose mouths extend broad outwash fans consisting of rocks, gravel, sand, and silt. These have been eroded from the mountain valleys and coalesce to form broad alluvial aprons. In places, lava flows and cinder cones lend variety to the landscape. Among the brown, vegetationless mudhills of the Mojave

Above : The aborigines of the Australian desert live entirely by hunting and gathering food. They wear no clothes, but their dark skins protect them from excessive ultraviolet radiation.

Left : Wallabies or small kangaroos that move by hopping – an adaptation to open country. When they sit upright the tail serves as a prop. They are chiefly to be found on the plains and desert of Australia where they feed on grass and small plants.

Above: Monument Valley, Arizona, a dramatic example of wind erosion.

desert in California may be found plates of weathered gypsum (hydrated calcium sulphate) and the White Sands of New Mexico are formed of almost pure gypsum from a dried-up lake bed.

These deserts owe their aridity to a number of conditions. Although the summer may be extremely hot, the winters are cool or cold especially in the Great Basin desert which lies between the Rockies and Sierra Nevada-Cascade ranges at an average altitude of 1500 m (5000 ft). The Sonoran desert of Arizona, California and Mexico is probably the best known of the American deserts. The Chihuahuan lies to the east, in New Mexico, Texas and Mexico.

The vegetation of the Great American deserts is of two general types, sagebrush and saltbush in the cooler portions, and mixed shrub and cacti and other succulents in the warmer portions. The southern deserts are often dominated by the creosote bush.

The fauna of the American deserts is unusually rich and includes the puma, jaguar, peccary, prong-horned antelope, and bighorn sheep, as well as a wide variety of smaller mammals, birds, reptiles, amphibians and invertebrates. The adaptations of many of these to desert life are described in the next chapter.

The Atacama desert

This is an arid, barren and saline region of northern Chile that covers most of the provinces of Atacama and Antofagasta, the Argentine territory of Los Andes and the south-western corner of Bolivia. Its higher elevations are known as the 'Puna de Atacama' and are continuous with the great *puna* region of Peru. The latter is a high, bleak and mountainous plateau in the Andes, with an altitude that ranges from 2100 to 4100 m (7000 to 13,500 ft). On its eastern side, occasional rain storms and streams from the melting snows allow a certain amount of vegetation to flourish but, elsewhere, the general aspect of the *puna* is barren and forbidding. The winters are cold and dry, the summers stormy. Much of the plateau is covered by occasional tufts of coarse grass, except where great saline lagoons and dry salt basins occur. The region has the world's largest natural supply of sodium nitrate which was formerly mined on a large scale. Westward, the land slopes towards the Pacific, and the coastal regions of the desert are rainless. The fauna includes small rodents such as the vizcacha and chinchilla; the huanaco and the smaller vicuña which inhabits higher elevations – both are New World relatives of the camel – and the giant Andean condor.

Left: Lava desert in the Andes near the pass of Huaitiquina between Chile and Argentina.

Above: The Andean desert of Chile, San Pedro de Atacama.

The Patagonian desert

An arid zone extends along the entire length of Argentina between the Andes mountains to the West and the Atlantic Ocean, and northwards into the Monte desert, and Gran Chaco. Winters are cool and summers mild in the Monte desert, but precipitation, which occurs mainly in summer, is generally less than 20 cm (8 ins). The climate of the Patagonian desert is cold, temperate, very dry and windy. Much of the Monte desert consists of muddy depressions, salt pans, dunes, badlands, brackish soils and tablelands covered with resinous bushes, many of which are totally or partially aphyllous – that is, without leaves, photosynthesis taking place in the stems of the plants. The terrain of the Patagonian desert consists of extensive plateaux, more than 900 m (3000 ft) high in many places, sloping towards the sea. The rivers flow through deeply incised, narrow valleys and the surface soils are mainly gravelly. The vegetation is dominated by widely spaced clumps of xerophytic grasses and low cushion-type shrubs. The aridity of the area renders it unsuitable for most fauna. The major Indian tribes were notable for their tall and athletic physique, but they are now rapidly disappearing as ethnic entities.

THE WORLD'S LOW LATITUDE DESERTS	Square kilometres	Square miles
Arabian Desert	2,600,000	1,000,000
Atacama Desert (Peru and Chile)	360,000	140,000
Australian Desert	3,400,000	1,300,000
Great American Desert (including the *Great Basin, Mojave, Sonoran* and *Chihuahuan* deserts of S.W. North America)	1,300,000	500,000
Iranian Desert (Persia)	390,000	150,000
Kalahari and Namib Desert (S.W. Africa)	570,000	220,000
Patagonian Desert (Argentina)	670,000	260,000
Sahara Desert	9,100,000	3,500,000
Takla–Makan Desert (including the *Gobi Desert* from western China to Mongolia)	520,000	200,000
Thar Desert (India and Pakistan)	600,000	230,000
Turkestan Desert	1,900,000	750,000

Desert Life

Although often thought of as desolate wastelands, deserts nevertheless harbour a varied and fascinating selection of animals and plants. While animals are largely dependent upon the vegetation, they also show peculiar adaptations to the rigorous conditions for survival imposed by desert life. These vary from their highly developed ability to conserve water to their coloration. Some desert animals, showing different colours to those they would in other regions, have adapted to their environment by being either yellow so as to be totally inconspicuous or black – which warns off would-be predators. Plants, too, show varied adaptations to desert life – the lithops, or stone-plant, for instance, resembles small pebbles effectively concealing it from grazing animals.

Desert vegetation

Most deserts and semi-desert regions support some vegetation although their climate and soils are so dry. Probably the least amount of plant life is found in areas of *hammada* or denuded rock, except where these are traversed by *wadis*. Although dunes are usually quite bare, sandy desert generally has a less scanty flora than *hammada*. The spacing of desert vegetation reduces competition between individual plants for the scarce resources of water.

Beyond the edges of true desert lie shrub-steppe lands where the rainfall is also very scanty. Such is the acacia desert-scrub extending south of the Sahara from Senegal, West Africa, to the Red Sea and Somalia, East Africa. Where there is moderate rain, even if it falls only in a few days of the year, grassland savanna is found.

Desert plants are adapted in various ways to withstand the adverse conditions under which they have to live. The ultimate stress suffered by desert plants is the dehydration of their protoplasm, and the amount of water that can be lost at the cellular level, before irreversible dehydration sets in, varies greatly in different species. In the creosote bush of North America the water content of the leaves may drop to 50 per cent of their dry weight, but the plant will recover when rain falls. (In contrast, the water content of the leaves of forest trees is usually in the range of 100 to 300 per cent of the leaves' dry weight.)

Root systems may be widely spreading, as in the saguaro cactus, or deeply penetrating, as in the mesquite tree, where they can reach a depth of over 50 m (164 ft). Succulent plants, such as cacti and euphorbias, store water in their stems. The barrel-cactus stores so much liquid in its stem that it has been used as an emergency source of water by Indians and other travellers in the American desert. Water-loss through evaporation is often reduced by evolving small, fleshy leaves, a thick, waxy covering, or a mat of downy hairs.

The Cactaceae is an American family, and the cacti of other continents have been introduced since the time of Christopher Columbus. There were no prickly pears in Israel when Jesus Christ was alive, and the artists who depict them in religious paintings are mistaken in doing so. However, many of the euphorbias, which are an Old World family, look very much like cacti because they have become adapted to desert conditions in the same way.

The Kalahari has a remarkable flora that includes many succulents, such as the mesembryanthemums or 'ice-plants' and the unique lithops or stone-plant. These tiny, pebble-like plants so

Left: The elf owl is not much larger than a sparrow. It inhabits the abandoned holes of desert woodpeckers in saguaro cactus plants and is only found in deserts where these plants grow.

69

closely resemble the stones among which they grow that they are difficult to distinguish. Their camouflage no doubt protects them from grazing animals and their rounded shape reduces the area exposed to drying winds.

Some desert succulents store water in their leaves rather than in their stems. The yuccas and agaves of America and the aloes and mesembryanthemums of Africa do this, as do many salt-tolerating species that grow round the edges of *playas* (basins which become shallow lakes after heavy rainfall). The yuccas and aloes resemble each other closely, as do some cacti and euphorbias. In fact, the Joshua tree yucca of the Mojave desert, California, is, except for its flower, almost identical in appearance to a tree-like aloe of the Namib. Such examples of convergence are com-

mon among desert plants as well as animals.

The agaves have rosettes of large, fleshy, and often spiny leaves. Only two or three leaves are formed each year but, after many years, a gigantic flowering stalk shoots up, sometimes reaching 6 m (20 ft) in height. When the flowers have set, the plant dies. Because of this peculiar life-cycle, the agaves are sometimes known as 'century-plants'.

Another extraordinary plant, the welwitschia of the Namib desert, has two enormous curling leaves, split longitudinally into strips, on which fog and dew condenses, providing water for the shallow roots.

Desert plants can be further divided into: drought-escaping ephemerals, which germinate and flower rapidly after rainfall; drought-evading plants which are so small that they conserve the little water available through their restricted growth; drought-enduring species, like the creo-sote bush, which cease to grow when soil moisture is absent; and drought-resisting succulents which hold reserves of water in their tissues.

Ephemeral plants, which spring up after rain, are partly responsible for the miraculous trans-formations of the desert landscape. The bare ground is quickly carpeted with green grass and flowering plants, often of astonishing beauty. A mass of evening primrose flowers covers the sand of the Californian desert in spring, briefly filling the air with their delicate fragrance before they wither and die. In the northern Sahara the barren ground becomes studded with blue convolvulus, yellow dandelions, red vetch and white daisies

Right: The top two diagrams show Rose of Jericho curled up into a ball (on the left) and uncurled when it is in moist surroundings (right). The centre diagram is a section of desert grass leaf which is curled so that the amount of water lost by evaporation is reduced. The bottom diagram is a plan of the shallow, spreading rooting system of the saguaro cactus, an adaptation that obtains full benefit from light showers.

Centre right: Tufts of grass, growing in the sand, form the typical vegetation of the Patagonian desert of Argentina.

Far right: A giant African euphorbia. The succulent euphorbias, although unrelated to New World cacti, inhabit similar desert environments.

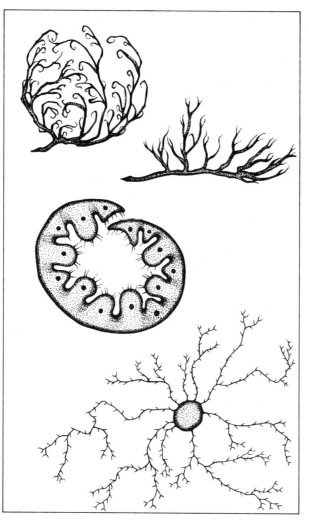

Previous pages: The organ-pipe cactus, unlike the saguaro, has many branches. The giant stems store water after rainstorms.

which produce quite an alpine effect in the bright sunshine. Leaves burst forth on naked trees and bushes, while flower buds swell among the thorns and spines.

The seeds of ephemeral plants have not only to survive years of drought and high temperature without losing their ability to germinate when rain falls, but they may also need to withstand strong concentrations of salt, formed by the evaporation of water. Finally, in a race against time, the whole life-cycle is compressed into a few weeks. Some plants even flower while they still bear their cotyledons or embryonic leaves.

Many kinds of drought-escaping plant produce seeds that are equipped with dispersal units to aid their distribution. In this way, the offspring have an increased chance of reaching a site that is suitable for germination. Others have evolved special mechanisms as a result of which stems, fruit-stalks, and other parts of the plant are closely curled towards one another when dry, but open when moistened. By this means, the seeds are scattered only in the moist season. This prevents dispersal of seeds from their parent plants, presumably already growing in a favourable locality.

Annual desert grasses often have well-developed dispersal mechanisms. A large number of

seeds become entwined to form a dense, rounded ball which is blown over the desert surface by the wind. As their sharp points come in contact with the soil, individual seeds become detached and anchored, until the ball finally disintegrates. Changes in the humidity of the air subsequently cause each seed to twist like a drill, forcing it even deeper into the soil, where it remains until rain falls. Individual seeds may also become hooked on to the hairs of animals – the legs of goats are sometimes completely covered with them – and are thereby dispersed. Many other plants of desert regions have well-developed barbs and bristles to aid their dispersal by animals, for example, the spikelets found in burr grasses.

The fruits of the colocynth are spherical, thin-walled gourds, about the size of an orange, which are blown about the desert and semi-arid regions of the southern Sahara sometimes for considerable distances until they become trapped against a rock or, more usually, in a hollow where eventually they disintegrate or become buried in wind-blown sand. When rain falls and collects in the hollows, the seeds germinate in favourable surroundings. Other rolling plants of the desert include the well-known 'Rose of Jericho'. As its fruits mature with the onset of the hot season, the

leaves fall off and the dry branches roll inwards forming a wickerwork basket. This protects the seed pods, until the branches uncurl again when next they become damp. The roots are small so that, when the plant is rolled up, it is easily detached by high wind and may be blown for a considerable distance. Some plants have spherical inflorescences or flowering shoots which, likewise, aid dispersal when they are rolled along by the wind. The fruit of one plant is shaped like a button with spiny seeds on its upper surface which become attached to the feet of animals.

A characteristic feature of most desert shrubs is the possession of painfully sharp and prickly thorns and spikes. The probable function of these is to afford protection against browsing and grazing animals. In the Australian deserts, where there is more vegetation as alternative food and, consequently, less grazing pressure, the acacias are less thorny than in the Sahara. Many desert plants, such as euphorbias, contain poisonous or irritant latex. Others secrete resins or tannins in the bark or leaves: the pods of the senna plant contain a strong purgative and the creosote bush has a pungent smell. Devices such as these render the plants unpalatable, both to mammals and to insects. They are especially important in desert regions, because food is so scarce that there is a much greater grazing pressure on the existing vegetation than is found in more luxuriant environments.

To a certain extent, spinescence is a consequence of drought, for the same plant growing in more humid conditions is far less spiny. This does not, however, provide a valid argument for disputing the fact that spines may have evolved as a result of grazing pressure in a dry environment. Since distasteful plants or animals have their own specialized predators, it is sometimes objected that there can be no selective advantage in the possession of an unpleasant taste or smell. Because the thorns of an acacia do not protect it from the browsing of goats and camels, or from the nibbling of caterpillars, it does not follow that the tree is not protected from a wide range of other potential enemies. The Sodom apple is eaten by one particular kind of grasshopper, but camels and goats will not touch it. In the same way, the aggressive habits, stings and distasteful qualities of ants fail to protect them from specialized predators such as frogs, toads, woodpeckers and ant-eaters; yet there can be no doubt that other predators are considerably deterred. The advantage conferred is not immunity, but relative

Above: Flowering cactus in the Colorado desert. The blossoms of the cacti are masterpieces of natural beauty and a striking feature of the American deserts.

Right : The Sodom apple is a characteristic plant of the Sahara. It continues to exist in regions where all other species have been removed by overgrazing, because it contains a bitter, poisonous latex.

Below : Alpha or esparto grass growing on a sand dune. Esparto grass is now grown widely in arid regions throughout the world. Its leaves are used for ropes, baskets, mats and making paper.

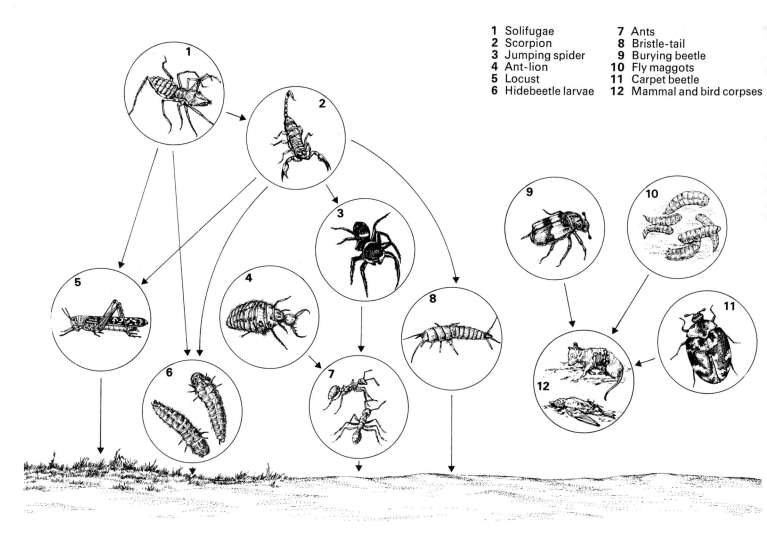

Above: Typical invertebrate food-chain in the desert, showing the predator–prey relationship of small animals (arthropods and reptiles).

freedom from attack. Furthermore, modern desert plants almost certainly have evolved under conditions less adverse than at present. The presence of a deterrent would then have been especially persuasive, for there would have been alternative food plants that did not possess it.

Animals of the desert

On account of their high reproductive potential, a quality which first impressed Charles Darwin with the inevitability of evolution by natural selection, living animals rapidly populate all available habitats, and there is continual pressure on them to exploit new ones. The conquest of the land has occurred independently within at least three separate groups: slugs and snails, arthropods, and vertebrates. Examples of all of these are to be found in the various deserts of the world. Adaptation to life on land presents animals with a number of physiological problems which become most acute in desert regions. These are associated mainly with effecting nitrogenous excretion and respiration while, at the same time, conserving water and preventing an excessive rise in body temperature. The greatest physiological problem which faces animals that live on land, and especially in arid regions, therefore lies in the

evaporation of water that inevitably occurs, especially during respiration. Small creatures such as insects, scorpions, spiders and other arthropods, have a very large surface area in proportion to their mass. Consequently, the conservation of water and the maintenance of a fairly constant internal medium are especially difficult for them. They can, to some extent, avoid desiccation by evolving a waterproof integument, but gas exchange must still take place. In contrast, larger animals, such as reptiles, birds and mammals, have a very much lower surface to volume ratio, so that water-conservation and respiration do not present them with such acute physiological problems. Size plays an equally important role in the temperature relations of animals.

The two main types of animal skeleton are directly related to the sizes of the animal. These are the exoskeletons of insects, arachnids, crustaceans, and other arthropods – the name arthropod refers to the jointed limbs of these forms – and the endoskeletons of vertebrates. An exoskeleton is basically a tubular structure, extremely resistant to twisting and bending but, above a certain size, exoskeletons become disproportionately heavy.

Arthropod size is additionally limited by the fact that animals encased in armoured skeletons

can grow only by moulting. After a certain size has been reached, linear dimensions increase only slightly at each moult, although the arthropod may nearly double its weight. In their design, the skeletons of vertebrate animals employ structural features which are related both to size and to locomotion. The capacity of a column to support weight depends upon its breadth. The leg bones of heavy vertebrates, therefore, tend to be relatively shorter and thicker than those of lighter species.

The influence exerted by the environment depends very largely upon the sizes of the animals that inhabit it. Very small animals are able to escape the rigours of life on land by living in microhabitats such as soil crevices, leaf litter, cracks in rocks, or the spaces beneath the bark of trees, where the evaporating power of the air is negligible or non-existent, temperature fluctuations are almost eliminated and the light is excluded. The animals that enjoy a hidden life in such secluded surroundings avoid desiccation mostly by means of behavioural responses which ensure that they spend most of their time in a moist environment. They are seldom found in deserts because suitable microhabitats are rare.

The fauna of any terrestrial region is largely dependent upon its vegetation. Some animals are able to live in areas of hot desert where even plants cannot grow. Their food chains are then based upon dried vegetation and grass seeds, often blown from a considerable distance. Dried vegetable matter is continually being transported by the wind into the more arid desert regions of the world. Part of this is eaten or destroyed immediately; the remainder becomes buried and, in the absence of bacteria, does not decompose but comes to the surface, often years later, when it supports a small population of insects and their larvae. Even vegetationless desert may therefore support a sparse fauna, provided that a sufficient concentration of dried plant material is present.

The problems confronting desert animals are concerned with the necessity to breathe, to conserve water and, at the same time, to avoid, tolerate or control extremes of temperature. Small animals have a very much larger surface area in proportion to their mass than larger ones. Consequently they cannot afford to use water for evaporative cooling. Arthropods (insects, spiders, scorpions and their allies) have relatively impervious integuments as do reptiles. They can therefore survive in deserts only by sheltering from the midday heat in bushes, cracks in rock or holes in the ground. Small mammals do the same. Birds, which cannot burrow, are at a great disadvantage in hot deserts. Larger mammals, although they also cannot burrow, have a smaller surface to volume ratio because of their size and can, therefore, afford to use water for cooling the body.

Survival in the desert

Insects Of the known terrestrial insects, surprising numbers are found in the desert. For instance, no less than 26 out of a total of 32 orders are represented in the north-west Sahara. In absolute desert the number is reduced to 14.

Bristle-tails are abundant sand-dwellers, commonly found under rocks or dried dung. They feed on dry vegetation and, in extremely arid regions, such as the Namib desert in south-west Africa, form the basis of a food-chain on which many carnivorous animals may depend.

Crickets, locusts and grasshoppers form an important element of the desert fauna and appear in abundance on the vegetation that springs up after rain. The desert locust is able to exist in the Great Palaearctic desert only as a result of its migratory habits. Solitary locusts of this species are normally found among sand dunes on coastal plains, scrub belts along the beds of *wadis*, in oases and similar habitats – islands of green vegetation in the barren desert. The migratory form of the desert locust appears when population densities build up. Long-distance movements of swarms take place high in the air where speeds are often greater than the speed of flight of the locusts. Consequently, it does not much matter in what direction the locusts are actually heading, for they inevitably get carried into areas of low barometric pressure where rain has fallen or is most likely to fall. Here they feed on the ephemeral grasses that spring up and, later, deposit their eggs. The female locust prefers to lay in sand that is dry on the surface but damp underneath, and the eggs do not develop unless they are kept moist.

Grasshoppers and crickets are also common throughout the deserts of the world. Whereas grasshoppers show little adaptation to their environment apart from possessing desert coloration, some crickets such as the 'sand-treaders' of North America possess combs of long hairs on their lower hind legs which enable them to make sure progress in sand. They lie buried during the day and emerge at night, especially in warm weather.

Many species of bugs live on the sparse vegetation of desert regions and the most conspicuous, the cicadas, are represented by several sand-dwelling species. Mealy bugs are also fairly

Left : The face of an ant-lion. These predatory insects inhabit burrows in sand while they are larvae ; the adults, which superficially resemble dragonflies appear on the wing at dusk.

Right : A group of African migratory locusts. From their outbreak area in the upper reaches of the Niger River in Mali swarms of these insects can, at times threaten the entire African continent.

numerous in desert areas and the 'manna', which sustained the Israelites during their travels in Sinai, was the secretion of one of them. Another, which occurs in arid parts of South America, becomes completely covered with a waxy coating in which condition it can resist prolonged drying for up to 17 years. When the cyst is put into damp soil, however, it absorbs moisture and continues its development.

Tropical termites usually extend their mounds in a north-south direction so that a comparatively small area of the nest is exposed to the midday sun. Dead shrubs in the Sonoran desert in California and elsewhere are usually eaten away by wood-eating termites, while others make their nests at the base of living agaves, ocotillo, cholla and other cacti. In the more arid deserts, only subterranean termites occur. Although earwigs are nearly always found in moist situations in temperate regions, some of the larger species are equally at home in quite arid places. Earwigs are nocturnal carnivores and hide under stones and in cracks in the soil during the day.

Ant-lions, whose larvae have been called 'demons of the dust', are characteristic insects of hot deserts during the summer season. Their cone-shaped pits can be seen especially well in fine sand. At the bottom of each pit lies buried an ant-lion larva, in ambush for passing ants and other insects that may fall into the trap. The prey is encouraged to slide to its destruction by particles of sand flicked with surprising force and accuracy by the larva waiting below.

Wasps and ants form a conspicuous element of the desert fauna. Bees require nectar and pollen and their activity is therefore restricted to the rainy season. Most wasp species are burrowers and excavate holes in sandy soil where they deposit the paralysed spiders and insects which

while blood-sucking horse-flies constantly attack camels, horses or donkeys. One of the bot-flies develops in the nose of the camel: the mature larva is sneezed out onto the sand where it pupates. 'Worm-lions' are larvae of certain flies which live in pits like the ant-lions to which they show a striking parallel in their behaviour.

Without doubt, darkling beetles are the insects best adapted to desert life. Second to them come dung-beetles and burying-beetles, while blister-beetles, ground-beetles and tiger-beetles are also strongly represented. The well-known Egyptian sacred scarab beetle acts as a scavenger by breaking up and burying the droppings of camels, goats and other animals. Many American scarab beetles have become secondarily adapted to eating vegetation and fallen leaves. Some of them may burrow to a depth of three metres (9.04 ft) or more in the soil. Predatory beetles are found on

serve as food for their larvae. The majority of ants live in subterranean nests although a few nest in the wood of dead trees or under bark. The primary adaptations of ants to life in the desert are related not so much to the dryness of the air as to the nature of the soil and the upkeep of their nests. Most of the species found in the Sahara, for example, live in comparatively moist localities and only a few are found in really arid soils. One species even brings water to its nest from the salty, damp sand of water-bearing strata deep underground. In a similar way, the harvester ants of California are susceptible to extremes of heat and cold, but live in deep nests and forage only during a brief period each day, when the temperature is favourable.

Butterflies and moths of the desert do not at first appear to show any special adaptations. A behavioural adaptation of small blue butterflies is their power of continued flight within the shelter of a small bush, even when the wind is raging outside. Hairy caterpillars are sometimes blown along by the wind, rolled up into a ball, while the larvae of certain species in America inhabit long tubes of sand attached to the stems of plants. Small moths are especially numerous in the American deserts. In most, the chrysalis is hidden underground, but the bag-worms are conspicuous because of the peculiar pupal cases they hang on desert plants.

Not only are flies, including the common house-fly, all too plentiful in the desert, especially near oases, but many other kinds also occur. These include sand-flies, crane-flies, hover-flies and long-snouted bee-flies which suck nectar and many of which are black in colour. Robber-flies and other predaceous species are not uncommon,

Left: Tiger beetles are fierce, day-active, predatory insects, which are characterized by their prominent eyes and large mandibles, (first pair of mouth appendages). The larvae are equally fierce and voracious.

Below left: A darkling beetle shamming death. These conspicuous, black insects form a dominant feature of the insect fauna of the Great Palae-arctic Desert. Protected by an offensive smell, the long-lived beetles have few natural enemies.

Bottom left: One of the few day-active insects of the Sahara this species of darkling beetle feeds mainly on dead insects but will also take some vegetable matter and dung. Like most of its relatives, it is incapable of flight.

Above: A robber-fly feeding on a yellow pansy butterfly. Adult robber-flies are predatory, feeding on a variety of other insects.

by evaporation, for the breathing holes or 'spiracles' open into it. Darkling beetles are omnivorous, feeding on vegetable matter, carrion and dung.

Arachnids Of all animals the scorpion is, perhaps, most symbolic of the desert, even though some kinds occur in the wet tropics, and others in temperate regions. Nocturnal in habit, scorpions spend their days in sheltered retreats. In North Africa, they are usually found under rocks and stones in shallow scrapes which they dig with their claws. South of the Sahara, however, where climatic conditions are more extreme, they inhabit deep burrows under rocks and at the roots of trees and shrubs. In Arizona, certain species dig down for a metre or so (three feet) into sandy wastes and river banks, while others in North Africa are equally enthusiastic excavators, making use of their enlarged pedipalps or claws for the purpose.

Scorpions are strictly carnivorous: they do not usually go far to seek their food, but tend to wait for the insects that enter their lairs. When hungry, however, they may emerge at night and walk about with claws extended, ready to grip the prey which may be subdued, if necessary, with the sting. There are two types of scorpion poison: one is local in effect and comparatively harmless to man, the other is neurotoxic and resembles the venom of vipers in that it has a haemolytic action and destroys the red blood corpuscles.

Solifugids are even more typical animals of the desert than scorpions. Sometimes known as 'jerrymanders', 'false-spiders', 'wind-scorpions' or 'camel-spiders', the long-legged species are familiar to all who have travelled in arid regions. A large camel-spider, whose formidable appearance is enhanced by its hairiness and bulk can, with its limbs, span a width of 12 to 15 cm (4 to 6 ins). These creatures avoid fertile oases and seem to prefer utterly neglected places where the soil is broken and bare. Sometimes they run so fast that they look like balls of yellow thistledown blowing over the desert.

As their name indicates, most solifugids are nocturnal and hide away in deep burrows or under stones during the daytime. They are exclusively predatory and have an extraordinary voracity: they will continue feeding until their abdomens are so distended that they can scarcely move. Almost any insect, spider, scorpion or other 'camel-spider' as well as small lizards, birds or mice, may be attacked and eaten. The adaptations of solifugids to desert life include considerable powers of water-conservation, the ability to tolerate extremes of drought and temperature, nocturnal habits, and a wide range of diet.

dung or carrion where they prey on the maggots and other insect larvae developing there.

Blister-beetles, on the other hand, are vegetarian. They secrete a disagreeable, oily fluid from the joints of the limbs which contains cantharidin and raises painful blisters on the skin. The adults possess conspicuous warning coloration, vivid black and green, brown or blue and red. Tiger-beetles and ground-beetles are predatory, both as larvae and adults. The latter seldom take to wing, but the former are skilful fliers, common on sand on the banks of rivers and temporary rain-pools, or beside the sea. The larvae inhabit tubes in the sand from which they watch for passing prey. In one American species, the sand grains are cemented with saliva and the burrow serves as a pitfall to trap other insects. Many of the desert ground-beetles are wingless. Particularly striking are certain gigantic nocturnal predators of the Palaearctic fauna. These have a conspicuous black and white warning coloration which is associated with an evil flavour.

Black darkling beetles are common in all the deserts of the world. They are able to live on dry food without any water. The majority of them are crepuscular or nocturnal, but one or two species may be day-active, except in extremely hot conditions when they burrow in the sand. Some species of the Namib desert have exceptionally long legs while others have very short legs and are adapted for burrowing. The commonest American darkling beetles are often active during the hottest parts of the day. Wings are usually absent in darkling beetles and the wing-cases are fused. The air-space beneath these not only serves for purposes of insulation, but it is of even greater importance in reducing the amount of water lost

Of the remaining orders of arachnids, only the spiders and mites are important inhabitants of the desert. Desert species are usually white or pale in colour without the markings found among their relatives that live in humid climates. Some of them have brushes of hairs on the undersides of their limbs which facilitate movement on sand. At least one species of hunting-spider that inhabits the Namib desert digs a tube in the sand and cements the grains with a criss-cross of webbing. Loose sand is pushed up the slope of the tube by the mouthparts of the spider. Others live on the trunks of acacias and other trees.

Crab-spiders lie in wait for their insect prey on the ground or in vegetation. They usually possess concealing coloration and match their background so closely as to be almost invisible. Some species can change colour quite quickly. The jumping-spiders are small animals with broad, square heads, extremely large eyes and short, stout legs. They have very keen sight and stalk their prey from afar whereas wolf-spiders hunt in the open and overcome their prey by speed and sheer strength. They have longer bodies and limbs, but their eyes are smaller. Cobweb-spiders construct funnel-shaped snares consisting of a triangular sheet with its apex rolled into a tube in which the spider awaits its prey. Orb-webs are usually attached to vegetation. One common inhabitant of sand dunes in the Mediterranean region has an extremely large web, but the spider has an irregular shape which, combined with its sandy colour, renders it inconspicuous.

Mites are sometimes found in desert soils, but they are not numerous. Adult giant velvet mites often appear in the deserts of Africa and America a week or two after rain, and probably feed on termites and other insects. They dig burrows where the sand is damp. Their scarlet coloration has a warning function and is associated with the possession of glands which secrete a fluid distasteful to enemies such as scorpions and 'camel-spiders'. The larvae are parasitic on grasshoppers. Many ticks are well adapted to life in arid places. When not attached to their hosts, they, too, show remarkable powers of water-conservation, and some can live for ten years or more without food or drink.

Amphibia Amphibians cannot be successful desert animals because they all need water in which to breed. A number of toads do, however, manage to maintain themselves in arid regions. Their physiological adaptations include reduction in evaporative water-loss and increased water-

Above: This species of scorpion is extremely poisonous and dangerous even to man. It is widely distributed in Algeria, Morocco and the western Sahara.

absorption after dehydration. In some species, the movement of water is more pronounced through the skin, while in others it is through the bladder. Both of these processes are under hormonal control. The eggs of desert toads that breed in temporary rainpools have the ability to develop extremely rapidly, so that the period of their dependence on water is reduced to a minimum. In dry weather, desert toads bury themselves deep in the soil so that they are protected from desiccation.

Reptiles Agamid lizards are widely distributed throughout the deserts of the Old World. They are terrestrial in habit, flattened in shape and mostly feed upon insects and spiders. Some species, in particular the scaly-tailed lizards, may be entirely herbivorous. In these the short, thick tail is covered with whorls of large scales while the body is much flattened and the head smooth and covered with very small scales. True lacertid lizards are also extremely common throughout the deserts of Asia and Africa. Many of them show a marked adaptation to desert life.

Iguanid lizards appear to fill a similar ecological niche in America to that occupied by the agamids of the Old World. Again, most species are insectivorous, but a few appear to be largely herbivorous. The 'horned toads' have flattened bodies covered with spiky scales. The desert iguana is abundant in valleys and plains where creosote bushes occur with rodent holes and burrows beneath them. Adaptations of the iguanid lizards include elongate, valvular scales fringing the edges of certain toes thus widening them, serving as sand-shoes and assisting movement beneath the surface of the sand. Nasal valves restrict the entry of sand into the nasal passages which, in turn, are specialized by being convoluted and having absorbing surfaces which reduce loss of moisture through the nostrils. The head is wedge-shaped to assist in sand swimming, which is further aided by the enlarged lateral scales on the legs and tail. These tend to force the animals down into the sand when the limbs are moved. Similar adaptations are found among desert-inhabiting members of other lizard families.

In many sand-dwelling lizards, including skinks and geckos, the eyes show a remarkable modification in the form of a window in the lower eyelid. In some species this takes the form of a circular, transparent disc. This occupies the whole eyelid which is permanently closed and fixed with its fellow, thus providing protection from the sand.

Geckos are widespread throughout the tropics and a number of species have become adapted to desert life. The heads of these lizards are broad, their bodies flattened and their toes equipped with pads which adhere by means of friction, thus enabling the animals to run up smooth, vertical surfaces. In some desert species the feet are webbed for support on loose sand. Most geckos are active at dusk and during the night, a behavioural adaptation of especial value in hot, dry

Above left: The jaws of the camel-spider are, in relation to its size, the largest and most formidable in the animal kingdom. Despite their ferocious appearance, these interesting animals are quite harmless to man.

Above: Few insects come amiss to the greedy camel-spider, seen here devouring a grasshopper nymph. Camel-spiders are among the few animals that will crack and eat a darkling beetle.

climates. One, however, which is common on both sides of the Mediterranean, although usually active in the evening, sometimes basks in the sun and comes into the light to catch insects. Geckos are able to withstand considerable desiccation and starvation, and one Saharan species may lose over half its body weight without ill effect and then recover when food is again available.

Several quite unrelated kinds of desert lizard have adopted a snake-like form of locomotion. The body is covered with smooth scales which cause little friction and the legs may be reduced or even lost, so that movement through the sand is accomplished entirely by wriggling the body.

Perhaps the most imposing of desert lizards is the African monitor which may reach a length of one and a half metres (5 ft). It is a speedy and rapacious creature which will eat any other animal that it can overcome. Although a certain amount of water is lost by evaporation through the skin, perhaps ten times the amount formed by metabolism, it is doubtful if this contributes much to cooling the body. Small reptiles have a higher rate of water-loss per unit of body weight than larger ones.

Like lizards, desert tortoises avoid the heat of the sun by burrowing deeply in the ground. They scrape the earth loose with the forefeet, and turning round push it away with the carapace or 'shell'. Advantage is often taken of excavations by other animals such as ground-squirrels. During the morning and evening, when the air is cool, tortoises warm their bodies by basking in the sunshine. They do not normally drink because

Above: A desert monitor-lizard eating an egg. These large lizards have a reputation for ferocity and will eat any small creature that they are able to overpower and swallow whole.

86

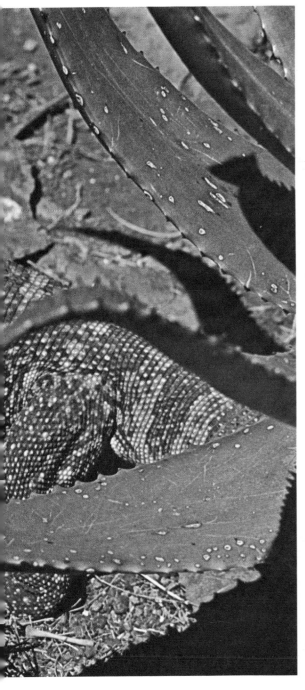

they can obtain enough moisture from the succulent plants on which they feed. They do, however, ingest large quantities when desiccated. The American desert tortoise exists without water throughout the entire dry season. Its eggs are laid in early summer and hatch in three or four months. Not until about five years after hatching do the young tortoises develop a hard shell and it takes them about 15 to 20 years to reach maturity.

The Greek tortoise occurs throughout the Mediterranean region and Asia Minor, its range extending eastwards as far as Iran. Although normally feeding on juicy plants where they occur, these tortoises have been found eating the astringent green fruits of dwarf palms. They spend much of the time basking in the sun but

seek the shade when their body temperature begins to approach lethal limits. At all times they rise late and retire early, being absolutely diurnal (day-active) in their habits. Evaporative water-loss from the African desert tortoise increases greatly when the air temperature exceeds 40.5°C (105°F) because the temperature of the body is maintained at this level by copious salivation which wets the head, neck and front legs. Thermoregulatory salivation occurs in all tortoise species that have been investigated. In the African species, the eggs are laid during the autumn and hatch the following summer at the time of the annual rains.

Snakes are much less common in deserts than lizards are. Nevertheless, they comprise an important element of the fauna. Snakes are the most

Top: A Mauritanian toad, which is one of the prettiest species of toads. It is found only in north-west Africa. It is active mainly at night and hides away during the fierce heat of the day.

Above: These giant velvet mites appear in the desert after rain, when they glut themselves on termites before retiring down their burrows until the next rainstorm, perhaps a year later.

highly specialized of the carnivorous reptiles, and are exclusively meat-eaters. Although their tolerance of high temperatures in general is lower than that of lizards or tortoises – for example the lethal temperature of the desert rattlesnake is 41.4°C (106.5°F) while that of lizards inhabiting the same area is from 45° to 47.5°C (113° to 117.5°F) – snakes are even more adept at insinuating themselves into holes and crevices. Like lizards, snakes possess relatively impervious skins which are especially impermeable in desert species and little water is used in excreting urinary waste matter. Their carnivorous diet is rich in moisture, and evaporation is greatly reduced by daily or seasonal quiescence in a relatively cool and humid burrow.

The two most important groups of non-poisonous snakes found in deserts are the worm-snakes and harmless colubrids. These snakes, having no special method of killing their prey, eat it alive so that it ultimately dies of suffocation or from the action of digestive juices. Worm-snakes have a tropical distribution, some of them extending into the desert where they lead secretive lives under logs and stones or burrow into the ground. Their eyes are rudimentary, their dentition reduced and they feed on termites and other small insects.

Desert colubrid snakes show some of the adaptations to burrowing in sand that are found among desert lizards, and are usually more slender than their relatives from more humid places. They are active creatures belonging to a vast assortment of species. In the related back-fanged snakes which are venomous, the prey has to be gripped before the poison, which usually has a paralysing effect, can be chewed into the wounds made by the teeth.

Dangerously poisonous desert snakes include the vipers and rattlesnakes whose poison causes collapse and heart failure and the cobras whose venom induces paralysis. True vipers are confined to the Old World, whereas rattlesnakes and a number of related types are found mostly in the New World with a few species in Asia. Both the horned vipers of the Great Palaearctic desert and the sidewinder rattlesnakes of the Great American desert propel themselves forward by looping their bodies sideways in S-shaped curves. The trail that is left in the sand is a ladder-like succession of furrows. Such spiral sidewinding causes the snakes to move obliquely in the direction to which the head is pointing. In this way the prey can be approached unobtrusively, and at the same time the area of the snake's body that touches the

Above: Foot of the Namib palmate gecko. Desert geckos often have wide feet like snow-shoes that stabilize them on the surface of the sand. They are not adhesive and cannot be used for climbing unlike other geckos.

88

Above: Worm snake in a termite nest. These secretive, burrowing snakes are found throughout the savanna and semi-arid areas of Africa and south-western Asia on the fringe of the desert. They feed on insects and are quite harmless to man.

Above left: The spiny-tailed desert gecko digs shallow tunnel systems or hides under rocks during the day. Its eyelids are fused and transparent but can be cleaned by the large flat tongue.

hot sand is reduced. The prey of desert vipers and rattlesnakes consists mainly of desert rats, jerboas and gerbils.

The Egyptian cobra is widely distributed throughout Africa and can be found as far south as Natal. It seems to prefer dry, sandy places where its brownish coloration blends with its dusty surroundings. A quick, irritable animal, it rears up at the slightest disturbance and strikes with loud hissing. It moves its body in a series of horizontal waves which flow continuously from head to tail, while its body presses against the ground, so that it seems to move without effort.

Birds Compared with most other animals, birds show little specialization of form or appearance for desert life. Apart from being generally paler in colour, most species are difficult to distinguish from their relatives of humid climates. The most numerous kinds are insect-eating species, followed by seed-eaters and, lastly, by carnivores. Many of the latter feed chiefly upon reptiles, and, for example, in the Sahara live to a large extent upon spiny-tailed lizards. The Sonoran white-rumped shrike impales its lizard prey on sharp thorns, while the American road-runner, a relative of the cuckoo, regularly feeds on snakes, as does the African secretary-bird.

Although many species of birds have been recorded from desert regions, their distribution there is usually closely related to the presence of surface water for drinking. Where there is no such water within their range of flight, birds are very scarce in contrast to reptiles and small mammals. Water-loss by evaporation is the most serious physiological factor limiting their distribution in arid regions. Most birds are active during the daytime and, because they do not have burrowing

habits, cannot escape from the midday heat as do small mammals and reptiles. Even though they rest in the shade as much as possible during the hottest part of the day, they are exposed to much more radiant energy than are burrowing rodents. Owls and nightjars are exceptional in hiding themselves in rock clefts during the daytime.

Most desert birds may be seen feeding actively early in the morning but, later in the day, the smaller kinds shelter in trees with hanging wings and open beaks while large species, such as eagles, hawks and vultures, circle high in the sky where the air temperature is considerably lower than it is near the ground. Carnivorous and insectivorous birds obtain plenty of water with their food: it is the seed-eaters that are faced with the greatest problem of survival. They are helped, however, by their normal high body temperatures and excretory metabolism which enables them to excrete a very thick and concentrated urine, containing considerable amounts of insoluble uric acid crystals. Birds lose water very much more rapidly than mammals of comparable size, however, and can survive only on very succulent food or by drinking daily.

Every morning, sandgrouse, which are related to pigeons, fly distances of up to 32 km (20 miles) from their desert feeding grounds in order to drink their fill from water-holes and rivers. Huge flocks of these birds, constantly calling to one another with their guttural cries, plummet into the shallow water, drink for two or three seconds, and then wheel off again into the sky, their rapidly beating wings twinkling in the sunlight as they go. In the breeding season the male bird, who is equipped with special water-absorbing feathers, ruffles his breast before drinking. When he returns to the nest he is thereby able to moisten the eggs, which prevents them from overheating. (Instead of incubating their eggs, most desert birds have to shade them from the scorching sunshine. Only those of the ostrich are large enough to survive unshaded for any length of time.) After the sandgrouse eggs have hatched, the male bird brings moisture to the young who pass his wet feathers through their beaks. Until they are old enough to fly, they do not obtain water in any other way.

Owing to their large size, ostriches cannot obtain shelter from the heat of the day in the manner of smaller birds, nor are they so mobile. Although they must drink or eat very succulent food, nasal salt-excreting glands enable them to live off brackish or even salty water. Like camels they can withstand a loss of 25 per cent of their body weight, most of which can be replaced in a single drink. Cooling is achieved by panting, but

to range widely for food. The need to regain the safety of their burrows at short notice has engendered the evolution of speed.

Many desert mammals, including rodents, bats, hedgehogs, foxes, gazelles, and the addax antelope, possess greatly enlarged tympanic bullae. The significance of this common feature is not entirely clear, but it probably adds greatly to the sensitivity of the ear, especially to sounds of low frequency made by enemies such as owls and snakes. It may also aid in the perception of ground vibrations.

North American kangaroo-rats and other small desert rodents can survive indefinitely on dry food without any water to drink. Indeed, on an exclusive diet of dry grain, they can even gain weight. No physiological water storage is drawn upon, nor is there any increase in the concentration of the blood while living on a dry diet. This means that water is not conserved by the retention of waste metabolites, but the urine is almost twice as concentrated with respect to salts as is the urine excreted by the white rat and 1.6 times as concentrated with respect to urea. Kangaroo-rats are even able to utilize sea-water for drinking as they can excrete such large amounts of salt and yet maintain a normal water balance.

The amount of water lost by evaporation through the lungs is extremely low in desert

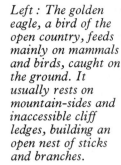

Left: The golden eagle, a bird of the open country, feeds mainly on mammals and birds, caught on the ground. It usually rests on mountain-sides and inaccessible cliff ledges, building an open nest of sticks and branches.

Below left: The secretary-bird, found only in Africa, is an inhabitant of open savanna or desert where it preys on all creeping things, notably snakes.

the animals allow their body temperatures to rise several degrees before they begin to pant. Thus, water is not used for evaporative cooling until this becomes absolutely necessary. The ostrich, a native of Africa and the Middle East, is not entirely a desert bird for it is found throughout Africa wherever the country is open and dry.

Mammals Unlike most birds, small mammals are able to avoid the midday heat of the desert by burrowing. Their physiological problems are therefore concerned more with water shortage than with temperature stress. Many of them can exist without drinking at all, the most remarkable being the jerboas and kangaroo-rats.

Large numbers of rodents inhabiting different deserts of the world have characteristics in common, although some of them are but distantly related. Except for the spring-hares of South Africa, they tend to be about the size of a small rat, with short fore legs and long hind legs adapted for jumping. The number of toes is often reduced, the tail long with a terminal tuft of hairs, and the gait characteristically bipedal. The short fore limbs are used for burrowing, the hind legs for jumping, while the body is balanced by the tail. Because of the open nature of the terrain and the poverty of the vegetation, these animals may have

Below : Senegal
and-grouse. These
small desert birds
have affinities with
pigeons, but they are
terrestrial in habit
and their general
coloration matches
the soil on which
they live.

rodents. This is achieved by reduction in the temperature of the expired air as it leaves the tip of the nose, so that less water is required to saturate it. Kangaroo-rats are nocturnal and do not emerge from their burrows during the day. Measurements of temperature and humidity recorded in their burrows showed that, although the air is not saturated, its moisture content is from two to five times as high as that of the atmosphere outside. Consequently, the rate of evaporation of water from the lungs is considerably reduced. This is of great significance, for if the animals were breathing the air outside their burrows with its low moisture content, the rate of evaporation from their lungs would exceed the rate of formation of metabolic water but, as long as they breathe the moist air in their burrows during the daytime, there is an ultimate gain in water.

Like birds, desert rodents do not sweat: indeed it seems likely that the general absence of sweat glands in small mammals results from the necessity to conserve water that is imposed by their relatively large surface area. In order to maintain a constant, normal body temperature when the air temperature is around 40°C (104°F), a kangaroo-rat would have to lose 20 per cent of its body weight per hour. But there is an emergency regulatory process for, if the body temperature approaches the lethal level of about 42°C (107°F), copious salivation occurs which wets the fur of the chin and throat. The cooling effect of this may keep animals alive for up to half an hour at temperatures fatal to other small rodents: but, because of the rapid heat-gain of small animals and the limited amount of water available, the time limit on the mechanism is severe. Possibly an animal driven from its burrow by a predator may have a better chance of survival with such a mechanism than without. Clearly, water can be used for heat regulation only in the greatest emergency and evaporation normally takes place only through the lungs.

The adaptations of the Egyptian jerboas to their desert environment are similar to those of the American kangaroo-rats. Underground living and nocturnality are partial solutions which jerboas have found to the three main problems of the desert – scarcity of water, rarity of food and excessive solar radiation. Jerboas and kangaroo-rats can live indefinitely on a diet of dry barley or wheat grains (containing 11 to 12 per cent water), by eating little and excreting little. The urine is concentrated and the faeces are dry.

Little is known about desert carnivores, but there is no doubt that they obtain considerable quantities of liquid from the blood of their prey. In addition, they tend to have a more varied diet

than their relatives from more temperate regions. Desert carnivores include foxes, jackals, hyaenas, coyotes, small cats, badgers, skunks, ferrets, some carnivorous marsupials and the Australian dingo. Of these, only foxes are found in extremely arid regions and they may be entirely independent of drinking water. The delightful fennec-fox of the Sahara exhibits several adaptive characteristics which are paralleled by the American kit-foxes. The fennec is much smaller than its relatives from temperate climates. It has well-developed sense organs, large eyes and ears, and spends the day in a deep burrow, thus avoiding extremes of heat. Like other desert species, it is a pale sandy colour. It is more catholic, too, than other foxes and lives mainly on insects, lizards, rodents, dates and so on. Its liking for sweet things provides an explanation of the fable of the fox and the grapes. If they get overheated, fennecs pant like dogs. They excrete a highly concentrated urine, and the same is probably true of kit-foxes. The young are born in burrows at the time of the spring rains.

A number of rodents and other small mammals are able to live in the desert by subsisting on moist food. These include the sand-rat of North Africa which lives and nests in places where the vegetation consists of succulent plants. These are usually extremely salty, but sand-rats eat them in great quantities and secrete a copious urine which may be up to four times the concentration of sea-water. The American pack-rats and ground-squirrels, which feed on juicy cholla fruits, do not possess the same ability to eliminate large quantities of salt but, nevertheless, excrete a concentrated urine. Pack-rats protect the entrances to their burrows by piling up stones and pieces of prickly cactus.

Other small American desert rodents are grasshopper mice, so called on account of their insectivorous diet which provides them with all their water requirements. The desert hedgehog of North Africa also obtains water from its food while the crest-tailed marsupial mouse or mulgara, which inhabits the most arid central parts of Australia, lives predominantly on insects, supplemented by occasional lizards and small rodents. Like the grasshopper mouse, it is able to excrete in a relatively small volume of water the large amounts of urea which result from its carnivorous diet. In common with most other desert dwelling mammals, it is a pale sandy colour.

Although many desert hares and rabbits excavate tunnels and burrows, the American jack rabbits remain above ground and have no sub-

Above: The
Californian
kangaroo-rat is
similar in appearance
and mode of life to
the jerboa, because
it, too, inhabits a
desert environment,
but the two animals
are not closely
related.

terranean retreat. They are found in areas where no free water is available and depend upon the moisture obtained with their green food. It is not entirely clear how they can survive in the desert, but the suggestion has been made that their very large ears, with a network of blood vessels, may serve to radiate heat to the sky while the animals are resting in the shade. Large ears are a characteristic of many desert animals and the Saharan hare also has ears much larger than those of its relatives of temperate climates.

The larger mammals of the deserts of the Old World include antelopes, gazelles and wild asses. In the arid regions of North America, their ecological niche is occupied by the pronghorn formerly very common in the prairies but now extremely rare, and the mule-deer. The larger herbivores of the Australian deserts are marsupial kangaroos and wallabies, whose young are born at an early stage of embryonic development and carried by the mother in a pouch or marsupium until they are big enough to fend for themselves.

None of these animals is able to escape the rigours of the desert climate by burrowing, but they have low water requirements, and their mobility enables them to travel long distances to obtain drinking water. The dorcas gazelle, one of the smallest of the gazelles with a shoulder height of up to 60 cm (23.4 ins), is widely distributed throughout the Sahara desert. The back and sides are sandy reddish-brown, the belly white, the two colours being separated by an indistinct dark stripe. The horns of the male are stouter and more curved than those of the female. In Morocco, Palestine and other desert regions of the Mediterranean basin, dorcas gazelles do not require water and can obtain sufficient moisture for their needs from succulent roots and plant material. In the Sudan, however, they feed on acacia leaves which contain nearly 50 per cent of free water, but lose weight steadily on dry food when deprived of water. After five days' desiccation, up to 1.5 litres (2.63 pints) of fresh water can be ingested and smaller quantities of saline water are taken. With increasing dehydration, the body temperature tends to fluctuate and there is some degree of hyperthermia or increased temperature as is found in camels, the urine becomes concentrated, faecal pellets become smaller and drier, and food intake is reduced. Feeding ceases when about 15 per cent of the normal body weight has been lost, and the animals appear weak and emaciated. This may take up to 12 days in winter but, in summer, gazelles cannot survive on dry food for more than

five days without drinking. It seems that, whereas camels are able to survive on a low water intake, the physiological adaptations of the dorcas gazelle are not so well marked and their survival depends upon speed and mobility so that they can travel great distances to water. Gazelles can run at up to 85 km.p.h. (50 m.p.h.). They migrate from the western Sudan to the Nile during the dry season. During the rains, herds of two dozen or more can be seen but, in dry weather, they are more solitary. In very hot weather, they have been seen to cool themselves in the Red Sea, but they do not drink salt water. A dwarf race of the Arabian gazelle, one-third of the normal weight, is said to inhabit islands in the Red Sea where no fresh water is available for drinking.

The saiga antelope which roams the arid plains of western Asia is about the size of a fallow deer. Its coat is dirty yellowish in summer, and longer, thicker and paler in winter. In common with other animals of steppe and desert, where concealment is scarce and sources of water infrequent, it is speedy and can cover long distances.

Among the most interesting of the hoofed mammals of the African and Asian deserts and steppes are the wild asses. Several species are known, including the onager of which different subspecies occur from Central Asia to north-west India, Baluchistan, Iran and Syria. This is the 'wild ass' of the Bible: it is white with a large yellowish area on each flank and a black dorsal stripe, mane and tail. It is gregarious, the herd being led by an old stallion. The kiang is a deep reddish-brown in colour and is more solitary. It inhabits the high desert plateaux of Tibet, Ladak and Sikkim. The kulan extends from the steppes of Transcaspia, Transbaikal and Mongolia into the Gobi desert. African wild asses are represented by the Nubian and Somali races. Probably none of the wild asses of today are pure descendants of the original, true wild ass, for there has been much interbreeding with domestic asses.

Asses are sure-footed, long-eared animals that almost rival the camel in their ability to tolerate a considerable degree of dehydration and to withstand a water-loss of 30 per cent of body weight. Their drinking capacity also is impressive and within a few minutes they can ingest more than a quarter of their body weight. Asses appear to lose water more rapidly than camels, however, because the fluctuation in their body temperature is smaller. Their fur coats are thinner and provide less effective insulation and their behavioural adaptations which reduce heat-gain from the environment are less extreme.

The Australian red kangaroo and other species range widely throughout the inland desert regions of the continent. They can exist on the water content of their vegetarian diet supplemented by infrequent drinking. Their bipedal, leaping gait in which the body is carried well forward and counterbalanced by the massive tail enables them to travel at 30 km.p.h. (18.6 m.p.h.). In short bursts a speed of 50 km.p.h. (31 m.p.h.) can be achieved with leaps of over 7 m (23 ft). Panting is the major avenue of evaporative heat-loss in red kangaroos. Sweating is more important to them than it is to the hill kangaroo, which shelters during the day in rocky outcrops and caves where the humidity is high. Differences in the insulation and reflection properties of the fur in the two species have also been found to be related to differences in their habitats.

The quokka is a medium-sized marsupial, about the size of a rabbit, which inhabits the offshore islands and coastal regions of south-west Australia where no fresh water is available and moisture obtained from the vegetation is supplemented by sea-water. In hot weather, the body is cooled by sweating, supplemented by copious salivation, licking of the feet, tail and belly, a trait also found among kangaroos.

Camels are large, even-toed ungulate mammals with humped backs and digitigrade feet in which there are only two toes, the third and fourth. These are united by thick, fleshy pads which prevent them from sinking in soft sand and are tipped with nail-like hooves. Camels were first domesticated by man in prehistoric times. Two species are recognized: the Arabian camel or dromedary which is widespread throughout the Middle East, India and North Africa and possesses a single hump, and the bactrian camel. The latter is a heavily-built, two-humped animal which inhabits the deserts of central Asia where the winters are cold. It has a longer, darker winter coat, short legs and seldom measures more than 2.1 m (6.9 ft) from the ground to the top of the humps. This is about the height of the shoulder in the taller and more slender dromedary.

The dromedary is known only in domestication, but the small humps and feet and short, brown hair of the bactrian camels of the Gobi desert indicates that they are genuinely wild and not merely feral – that is, descendants of domesticated stock that have escaped over the centuries.

When moving at speed, camels pace. Like the giraffe and brown bear, they raise both legs on the same side of the body and advance them simultaneously whilst the weight is supported by the legs of the opposite side. In this way a speed of up to about 8 km.p.h. (5 m.p.h.) may be achieved.

Although they chew the cud, camels differ from true ruminants in that they lack an omasum

or third section to their stomachs. The smooth-walled rumen or anterior section has small sacs or diverticula leading from it. These were formerly called 'water sacs' because of an erroneous hypothesis, dating from Pliny's *Historia Naturalis*, that they served the function of water storage. These glandular rumen sacs contain a fluid having the same salt content as the rest of the body. It looks like green pea soup and is quite repulsive. To the desert traveller who has no water, however, any fluid is attractive. The many tales of people who have saved their lives by killing their camels to drink the fluid in the rumen sac may therefore be true.

Equally erroneous is the idea that the camel stores water in its hump, or that the fat from which the hump is composed is essentially a water store itself. On oxidation, this fat produces metabolic water, but the extra oxygen that must be used in the process involves, in turn, an extra loss of water through the lungs which just about cancels any gain from oxidation of the fat. The camel's hump is actually a food store, which, by being concentrated in one large depot and not distributed as a layer of subcutaneous fat, allows the rest of the body to act as a radiator for cooling purposes. In Zebu cattle a fat deposit also lies in the hump, but in desert sheep it lies in the tail.

The rate of urine flow is low in camels and little water is lost with the faeces. Instead of eliminating all the urea produced in metabolism the camel, like ruminants, can utilize it for microbial synthesis of protein. In this way the amount of water excreted is reduced and greater use made of the food.

The coarse hair on the camel's back acts as a barrier to solar radiation and slows the conduc-tion of heat from the environment. It is, however, ventilated so that the evaporation of sweat occurs on the skin where it provides maximum cooling. At the same time the camel avoids undue water-loss by allowing its temperature to vary over a range greater than that of other mammals and sweating does not begin until the body temperature has risen to $40.7°C$ ($105.3°F$). Thus heat is stored during the day and lost at night when the environmental temperature is lower. Moreover, when the camel's temperature rises the difference between it and that of the air is reduced so that less sweat is required to prevent a further increase in body temperature.

The camel can tolerate a much greater depletion in body water than most other mammals and may, without ill effects, lose about 30 per cent of its body weight (100 kg out of 450 kg or 220 out of 990 lbs) as compared with about 12 per cent in man. It also has an unusual drinking capacity and can assimilate 115 litres (25 gallons) or more in a very short space of time. The blood and tissue fluids become rapidly diluted to an extent that would cause other mammals to die from water intoxication.

When most mammals are subjected to high temperatures in dry air, desiccation proceeds

Above left : The Saharan hare, like many other desert animals, has ears much larger than those of its relatives from temperate climates.

Above : The red kangaroo is the largest of Australia's kangaroos and stand as tall as a medium-sized man. It lives in herds, seeking sheltered, bushy places by day from where it comes out at twilight to feed.

wild game of Africa, including the buffalo, oryx, eland and black rhinoceros. The eland, in particular, can endure comparatively large variations in body temperature without sweating, thus conserving moisture. By eating succulent food and sheltering from the heat of the day, the eland counteracts the inevitable water-loss imposed on it by the arid regions that it inhabits. It has been estimated that about 4 litres of water per kilogramme (1 gallon per 2.2 lbs) per day are available to the eland without drinking, and the animal can maintain itself for long periods and travel great distances from water in search of its food.

Above: Female dorcas gazelles – the horns of the males are stouter and more curved. This Saharan species is one of the smallest gazelles.

teadily while the body temperature remains onstant. As water is lost through evaporative ooling, however, the blood gradually becomes nore viscous until it cannot circulate quickly nough to carry away metabolic heat to the skin. t this point the temperature suddenly rises and explosive heat death' results. In camels this is voided by a physiological mechanism which nsures that water is lost from the tissues only, vhile the blood volume remains fairly constant. 'hus, the adaptations of the camel to its desert nvironment do not involve independence of rinking water but, rather, the ability to econom- ze the water available and to tolerate wide ariations in body temperature and water content. n winter, when the temperature is comparatively ow and water is not needed for heat regulation, amels become independent of drinking water for everal months. In summer the length of time etween drinks depends on the environmental emperature and the activity of the animal.

Domestic animals, such as the ox, buffalo, heep, goat, pig, donkey and horse, also show ifferent degrees of variability in body tempera- ure. The camel is the most variable in this respect, he sheep most stable. Daily or seasonal changes n body temperature are also tolerated by other

Adaptation to life in sand

Many desert animals show adaptations for living in sand. Bristle-tails take refuge at the base of grass tussocks where they wriggle or almost swim with fish-like movements in the sand. At least one species of plant-sucking bug has the same habit, and several species of darkling beetles have become flattened and plate-like in appearance, with short legs and the body expanded into a thin, wide plate with sharp edges. They burrow rapidly into the sand with alternate sideways movements. Some of these flattened beetles, which feed on the leeward side of the dunes, orientate themselves horizontally so that the smallest digging move- ment of the legs starts a cascade of sand from above which covers them very rapidly.

In parts of the Sahara and other sandy deserts, many of the species associated with dunes and *ergs* show adaptations for burrowing. Some are modified to swim through a loose substratum without making a hole, some excavate pits and others mine tunnels in more cohesive sand. A number of insects and arachnids have enormous

brushes of flattened hairs or bristles on the undersides of their legs which act like snow-shoes and facilitate their movements through the sand.

The lizards of sand dunes and *erg* also show adaptations to the environment according to whether they are 'sand-runners' or 'sand-swimmers'. The former have the toes of the fore and hind limbs fringed with elongated scales. These presumably widen the surface which presses on loose sand, in the manner of snow-shoes. A modification that serves the same function is found in the duck-like webbed feet of a nocturnal gecko which lives in the sands of the Kalahari desert. In this animal, there is a complete webbing between the fingers and toes for support on loose sand. Dilations of the toes are probably also of use in burrowing. Lizards that live in sandy deserts are usually extremely rapid in their movements. When not running, they stand alert with their heads held high and the front part of the body raised on the fore limbs so that they clear the hot sand. In motion, the tail is held well above the ground as a counterpoise. Such adaptations are found in a number of unrelated families from different parts of the world.

'Sand-swimmers' include the skinks as well as other lizards and snakes which exhibit several profound modifications for rapid burrowing in loose sand. The nose is pointed or shovel-like, and some species can dive head first into loose sand as though it were water. The nostrils tend to be directed upwards instead of forwards and thus are protected from the sand. In most snakes, they are shielded by complicated valves, or are reduced to small pinholes. The eyes of the worm-snakes are overhung by large head shields. Lizards may have the lower lid much enlarged with a transparent window in it so that the eye can be closed without impeding sight, an arrangement carried to an extreme where the lower lid is fused with the rim of the reduced upper lid. The ear opening is also either small and protected by fringes of scales, or may even be absent in certain reptiles. Desert lizards and snakes often have widened bodies for burrowing by lateral and vertical movements instead of ploughing forward into sand. Sidewinding is found in snakes such as the American sidewinder and the horned vipers of the Great Palaearctic Desert. These snakes progress by lateral loops of the body which cause them to move obliquely.

Mammals may also show adaptations for life in sandy places. The camel, having lost all except two of its toes in the course of evolution, increases

Above: Dromedary feeding on saltbush in southern Tunisia The indispensable camel, known only domestication, originated in Arabi. but is now widespread.

he surface area of its feet by developing fleshy
ads which do not sink into the sand. Its eyes are
rotected by its long and abundant lashes and it
an close its nostrils at will to prevent the entrance
f sand. In the saiga antelope, the nostrils are
videly separated and turned backwards so that
and is excluded while the animal is grazing. The
ipedal gait of jerboas and kangaroo-rats, like
hat of marsupial kangaroos and certain desert
izards, is an adaptation for speedy locomotion in
pen country.

The most striking support for the hypothesis
hat the adaptations referred to here are, indeed,
orrelated with the sandy desert environment is
fforded by the extraordinarily close resemblance
etween unrelated animals occupying similar
cological niches in different areas of the world.
Examples are afforded by the kangaroo-rats of
America and the jerboas of the Old World deserts;
he jack rabbits of North America, the hares of
he Great Palaearctic desert, and the marsupial
quokka of Australia. The American kit-foxes are
uperficially very much like the Saharan fennec;
oad-runners of the New World, which are
elated to cuckoos, look like the coursers and
ratincoles of the Old World but belong to a
ifferent family of birds. There are marked

parallels between the iguanid desert lizards of
America and the Palaearctic lacertid lizards,
while the desert rattlesnake of Arizona, apart
from the possession of its rattle, is almost indis-
tinguishable from the horned viper of the Great
Palaearctic desert.

Daily behaviour patterns

Only a short distance below the surface of the
soil, conditions become less extreme in the desert.
Below 50 cm (19.5 ins) there is hardly any variation of temperature between night and day in the
desert sands while, at twice this depth, the annual
variation is below 10°C (50°F). A temperature
range of 30.5°C (86°F) has been measured on the
surface of the sand in southern Tunisia in April.
This range was reduced to 18°C (64°F) 5 cm
(2 ins) inside a cricket's hole, while 30 cm (11.7
ins) down the hole it was only 12.5°C (54°F).
From such results it can easily be seen that, by
burrowing, an animal can avoid the worst conditions of the desert.

An outstanding feature of the Saharan sands
that is of major importance to animal life is their
comparatively high humidity. Even during the
summer, the air surrounding loose grains at a
depth of 50 cm (19.5 ins) has a relative humidity

*Above: The
Bactrian camel has
two humps. Its legs
are shorter and its
fur thicker than that
of the dromedary.
This is an adaptation
to the cold winters of
Turkestan and the
Gobi desert.*

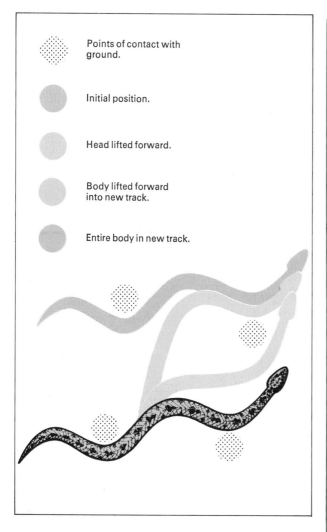

Points of contact with ground.

Initial position.

Head lifted forward.

Body lifted forward into new track.

Entire body in new track.

of 50 per cent. This moisture rises from extra-Saharan water which underlies most of the dunes. This occurs at a depth of 5 to 25 m (16 to 82 ft) in the Grand Erg Occidental. This is another advantage to burrowing animals because saturation deficiency, the evaporating power of the air, varies inversely with temperature so that extremes of both heat and drought are reduced underground. The exploitation of burrowing habits is by far the most important behavioural adaptation of small animals to desert conditions. Nocturnal patterns ensure that feeding, mating, dispersal and other activities take place during the hours of darkness when the air is comparatively cool and moist.

Burrowing and nocturnal habits are particularly marked in desert centipedes and woodlice which are not so well waterproofed as insects and arachnids. Nevertheless, even scorpions and solifugids, both of which are extremely resistant to evaporation, make deep excavations in the ground, the latter closing their burrows with a plug of dead leaves which helps to ameliorate the conditions inside. Some desert scorpions dig their holes to a depth of nearly a metre (three feet) but, in less extreme conditions, these animals are usually found during the day in shallow scrapes

under rocks which they dig with their claws. This must make life very much easier for them, but, even so, it is difficult to understand why scorpions and camel-spiders are so markedly nocturnal since, under experimental conditions, they can withstand remarkably high temperatures and severe desiccation. It is not easy therefore to ascribe any function, other than the avoidance of vertebrate animals, to their strict rhythms of activity. Of course, it might be argued that scorpions are protected by their poisonous stings. Poison is not always an effective deterrent to large and powerful enemies, however, which might well trample a scorpion underfoot just as deer will stamp on a snake. And it is well known that baboons and other monkeys become adept at catching scorpions without getting stung.

Above: A Namib desert sidewinder. These nocturnal vipers inhabit sandy deserts and feed on lizards, birds and small rodents. The diagram (left) show the sidewinder's unusual mode of movement which enables it to approach its prey in an unexpected way, while at the same time reducing to a minimum the area of its body pressed to the hot sand.

Above right : The scaly-tailed lizard is a common inhabitant of Egyptian oases. It is vegetarian, feeding on grass and other vegetable matter supplemented by insects. The young are insectivorous and their teeth are not adapted to a vegetarian diet.

Certain desert beetles, on the other hand, can often be seen wandering around in broad daylight. These are distasteful to predators however, and have extremely hard integuments. Their black coloration has a warning function and they are not compelled to be nocturnal in order to avoid predation. These are exceptional, however. Animals with moist skins, such as worms and slugs, or with porous outer coverings such as woodlice, centipedes, millipedes, certain mites, soft-bodied insects and amphibians, are usually only active at night, whichever part of the world they inhabit.

Most desert insects also confine their activities to the hours of darkness when the temperature is low and the relative humidity of the air comparatively high. This generalization applies even to species with comparatively impervious integuments and correspondingly lower levels of waterloss, whose relatives in temperate climates are normally active during the daytime.

Day-active insects tend to leave the sand when its temperature reaches about 50°C (122°F). Some climb grasses, some dive into holes, while others fly about above ground, making hurried landings to enter their burrows. When confined and prevented from burying themselves or flying away they very soon die. There are only a few animals, including some grasshoppers, beetles and spiders, that are active during the hottest part of the day in summer. Many of these have long legs which raise their bodies above the scorching sand. The same applies even to some nocturnal and crepuscular or twilight-active animals such as desert woodlice, dune spiders and darkling beetles.

Tortoises and many lizards are day-active, while most geckos and desert snakes tend to be nocturnal. Kangaroo-rats, jerboas, gerbils and other rodents, fennec and kit-foxes only survive in the desert because they are nocturnal. Birds, except for owls and nightjars, and large mammals, such as camels, antelopes and wild asses which cannot burrow, are day-active although, again, as

far as possible, they seek the shade when the sun beats down most fiercely.

Seasonal behaviour patterns

Like plants, many desert animals evade the adverse conditions of the desert summer by aestivating in a state of suspended animation. This dormant state or diapause is characterized by temporary failure of growth and reproduction, by reduced metabolism and enhanced resistance to heat, drought and other climatic conditions. During aestivation, the mouth of the shell of desert snails is closed by a thick diaphragm which reduces water-loss by evaporation. Desert snails have been known to remain in this state for over five years. The fauna of desert rainpools is dominated by filterfeeding crustaceans including tadpole-shrimps whose lifespan is compressed into a couple of weeks during which the eggs hatch, the animals grow to maturity and lay more eggs before the pools dry up. These eggs remain in diapause until rain falls again. Most desert insects and arachnids show diapause in one or other of their developmental stages, so that their period of maximum activity coincides with the time of rainfall which, though erratic, tends to be seasonal.

Although torpor has been described in only one bird, the poor-will, it occurs in a number of desert rodents such as ground-squirrels which aestivate during the summer or early autumn. Their body temperature then drops to that of the ambient air, respiration and other physiological processes being greatly reduced together with a corresponding water-loss.

Seasonal changes of the environment are reflected in the numbers and stages of development of the fauna so that populations of adults reach their peaks at the time of the rains. Certain adult darkling beetles, for example, begin to appear in small numbers during late October. Their population then gradually increases, reaching a peak in March. By the end of May the beetles have disappeared completely and only dead bodies can be found. During the hot season, the life-cycle is continued by the larval and pupal stages of development.

In the case of life-cycles such as this, which are extremely common among desert insects and arachnids, diapause and quiescence usually occurs in the developmental stages. At the time of the rains, the desert is transformed by an abundance of plant and animal life. Flowers are visited by bees, wasps, hover-flies, bee-flies and other insects. The droppings of camels and goats are rolled away by industrious beetles and grass seeds harvested by greedy ants. Termites extend their subterranean galleries to the soil surface and indulge in nuptial flights, while predators such as scorpions, camel-spiders, spiders, ant-lions, bugs, wasps, robber-flies and predatory beetles glut themselves on an abundance of food. With the rains, too, come swarms of locusts, which breed in the damp sand. The ephemeral vegetation is devoured by hordes of caterpillars and crickets, and the air buzzes with an abundance of flies, wasps and bees rarely seen at other times of year. Moths and butterflies are plentiful, migratory birds appear and build their nests, and most of the resident reptiles, birds and mammals produce their young while the harshness of the desert is briefly alleviated.

An interesting method of synchronization with environmental conditions is seen in the desert locust. Although the interval between fledgling and oviposition may be as short as three weeks in these insects, it can be extended to nine months. In Somalia, East Africa, for instance, delays of three to five months are quite common. Even after such an interval, however, egg-laying may occur more or less simultaneously at sites that are far apart. The obvious environmental factors with which this can be correlated is the onset of the rains, but maturation of the reproductive organs starts before the rains actually begin. The signal to which the locusts respond has been shown experimentally to be contact with the terpenoids of aromatic shrubs which are in highest concentration just before bud burst. In this way, the reproduction of the locusts is timed by the physiological rhythm of the vegetation. It is amusing that aromatic compounds such as terpenoids have probably evolved as deterrents to insects that would otherwise eat the leaves of the

shrubs that produce them. Their aphrodisiac effect on the locust is paralleled by their influence on humans for, in many countries, the scents of frankincense, myrrh and sandalwood are regarded as being extremely erotic.

Many species of birds inhabiting desert or semi-arid areas have adapted their reproductive physiology to take advantage of the unpredictable and sporadic rainfall. Breeding may be completely suppressed in rainless years and then take place, two or three times in quick succession, after a sudden downpour. In the desert areas of Arizona, Albert's towhee has been seen to nest within 10 to 14 days of heavy rain in March and April, and to continue breeding until late summer if rainy conditions prevail. A similar response to sporadic rainfall has been noted among many Australian desert birds, so that full breeding conditions are reached within a month of rain falling. In contrast, however, the sooty falcon of North Africa can breed under the harshest conditions.

The eggs of birds are vulnerable to overheating by exposure to direct sunlight. (Only the largest, those of the ostrich, can withstand prolonged exposure to the desert sun.) Various devices are therefore adopted to shelter them. Larks nest as far as possible in the shade of shrubs and bushes, wheatears in holes or small caves. Certain birds in Arizona and California are dependent upon holes hollowed out in the saguaro cactus by two species of woodpecker, and various other species use deserted woodpecker holes. These include the elf owl, screech owl, sparrow-hawk, and fly-catcher. Of the birds which breed in the open without protection, most kinds sit on their nests from the time the first egg is laid, so that it is never exposed to daytime heat or nocturnal cold. Pratincoles and terns are said to stand over their eggs, thus shading them from the sun.

Although the timing of the reproductive cycle in birds depends primarily upon day-length or 'photoperiod', breeding among desert species is frequently engendered in response to rainfall or the visual stimulus provided by green vegetation. It has been shown experimentally, however, that most desert birds can still be affected by variable 'photoperiod' although, under natural conditions, other stimuli may be stronger and override the influence of light. These opportunist breeders have also evolved the ability to respond quickly to suitable conditions so that the reproductive organs ripen much more rapidly than occurs in most temperate species. This is not always the

Above: Prairie rattlesnakes outside their den, which they have made from a prairie-dog hole. Even at birth, the button, easily recognized as the beginning of a rattle, is present. The sound acts as a warning enabling the snake to avoid conflicts and unnecessary use of its valuable poison.

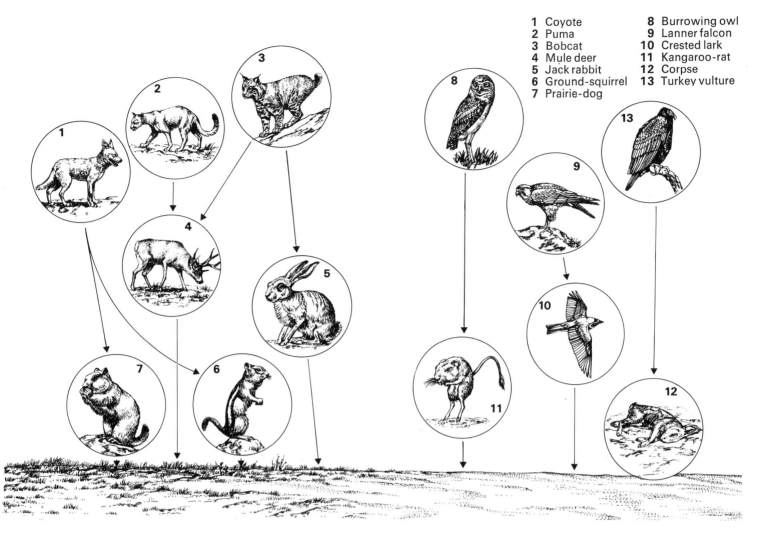

1	Coyote	**8**	Burrowing owl
2	Puma	**9**	Lanner falcon
3	Bobcat	**10**	Crested lark
4	Mule deer	**11**	Kangaroo-rat
5	Jack rabbit	**12**	Corpse
6	Ground-squirrel	**13**	Turkey vulture
7	Prairie-dog		

Above: An example of the food-chains in the North American desert. Carnivorous mammals and birds feed on herbivores which, in turn, are sustained by vegetation.

case however, for the double-banded courser breeds continuously in South Africa regardless of weather or season.

A similar situation manifests itself with mammals. In the matter of reproduction, desert mammals show some interesting adaptations, whose function is to ensure that breeding and the production of young occur at the right season. In Israel, both the rutting of camels and the time of birth, which takes place after a gestation period of 12 months, coincide with the short flush of green vegetation that appears from January to March each year. In most mammals the breeding rhythm is largely controlled by environmental factors so that, when transported from the northern to the southern hemisphere, they soon adapt their breeding cycles to the reversed conditions. In camels, however, the rhythm appears to be more firmly fixed. When camels from an area of winter rains are transported to deserts in which there is summer rainfall, they cease almost entirely to reproduce. Certain North African gazelles respond similarly.

It is difficult to see the advantage of having such rigid rhythms, and they are not characteristic of all desert mammals. In a good year, for example, some gerbils are capable of continuous

breeding although their reproduction is usually confined to the short spring and seems to be triggered by abundant fresh food. Seasonal reproductive rhythms are upset by irregular rainfall or drought. In the semi-desert of northern Kenya, where rainfall is very unreliable, the naked mole-rat (so-called because it is hairless) lives in colonies which greatly extend their burrows during the rains. Food is harvested collectively and stored at social nesting sites. Breeding follows the stockpiling of food upon which the females and young are very dependent. It is probable that no breeding takes place in very dry years.

Adaptive coloration

Most of the animals that live in desert regions are either buff, sandy or reddish-grey in colour – so that they resemble the ground on which they live – or else they are black. This applies to insects, scorpions, camel-spiders, reptiles, birds and mammals. Furthermore, the colour tends to be uniform, without pattern on the upper surface. The horned lark, cream-coloured courser, dorcas gazelle and oryx antelope of the Great Palaearctic desert have blackish markings on the head. So does Temminck's courser and the gemsbok of the

Kalahari, Botswana, but such patterns are exceptional. In contrast, the under surface of desert mammals is often white and the ventral surfaces of birds, reptiles, insects and arachnids are characteristically pale.

This type of coloration is widely distributed throughout the animal kingdom. The traveller who visits arid regions of the world will look in vain for the brilliant green colours which distinguish the fauna of the forest; nor will he find the immaculate white to be seen among polar birds and mammals – for animals often obtain protection from their enemies by closely matching the backgrounds against which they live. Such concealment is enhanced by having pale ventral colours so that the effect of shadow is obliterated. In deserts, concealing coloration is especially well marked, and different races of desert birds or mammals closely match their background. For example, the rodents which inhabit light soils and white gypsum sands of the Chihuahuan desert of New Mexico are extremely pale coloured, while their relatives from nearby lava beds are almost black.

In the northern parts of Algeria which fringe the Mediterranean, the crested larks are quite dark in colour. In the semi-deserts further south however, they are replaced by a paler race, while across the Atlas mountains are found crested larks so very pale that they closely match the colour of the desert sand and are easily overlooked when they do not happen to be on the wing or singing. Between Laghouhrat and Ghardaia a reddish form of crested lark is found, whose distribution corresponds fairly closely with the reddish, stony desert found in that region of Algeria. Similar examples have been cited from many other species of desert birds and mammals. Among reptiles and insects too, many cases are known of colour races which harmonize closely with the prevailing hues of the particular regions they inhabit.

Although many desert animals are exceptionally inconspicuous, the theory that desert coloration has been evolved as a protection against predatory enemies has not been accepted by all zoologists. One of the reasons for this is that many desert animals are nocturnal in habit, and it has been argued that concealing, or 'cryptic' coloration would be of little use to an animal that only ventures abroad in darkness. In the clear desert air, the stars shine very much more brightly, however, than they do in the humid regions of the world, and one can even read a book by moonlight. Under such conditions, cryptic coloration may well provide valuable protection from nocturnal carnivorous predators.

Some zoologists have argued, and not without evidence, that desert colours appear as a physiological response to the climatic factors of heat and droughts. This may well be the case, but it does not invalidate the assumption that pale colours, whatever the mechanism by which they are produced, may serve a very valuable function in assisting their owners to avoid enemies at night. For this reason, they must have been favoured by natural selection and become incorporated in the genetic constitutions of the animals that exhibit them. Whatever the background colour, cryptic desert animals tend to resemble it. In lava deserts, they are usually black.

Cryptic coloration can be remarkably effective for concealing animals, even where the ground is absolutely bare. For example, it is almost impossible to detect cream-coloured coursers or Egyptian nightjars before they fly, despite the comparatively large size of the birds. Likewise, when American desert rattlesnakes or Saharan horned vipers lie half-buried in sand, flush with the surface, they are nearly invisible. Of course, their camouflage is effective only when the animals are completely still, but the possession of concealing coloration is combined with the ability to remain motionless for long periods.

Cryptic desert grasshoppers often have their bodies widened and flattened in such a way that

the animals are triangular in cross-section and flat below. When they press their ventral surfaces to the ground, there are no shadows to betray them. In this attitude, every visible part of the insects is the colour of the desert and their bodies are roughened to resemble rough rock or sand. These insects also exhibit what is known as 'flash coloration'. When they move, they reveal a patch of brilliant blue or red in the hind wing which is covered when they are at rest. It is generally believed that such flash colours serve to confuse or misdirect enemies in pursuit of prey, for it is easier to mark the exact spot where an insect has alighted if its colour does not immediately change. The sudden disappearance of the flash coloration, combined with the equally sudden suspension of movement, misleads the eye and renders the animal's exact whereabouts all the more difficult to detect.

Certain desert insects attain a silvery or sandy appearance by being clothed with hairs of that colour. The phenomenon has been evolved on a number of separate occasions and is found in many bees, wasps, and flies. The fact that it has appeared in a divinity of insects indicates a common function and, indeed, it renders the animals almost invisible on the glittering sand and pale vegetation which they haunt. At the same time, the high reflectivity of the hairs probably lessens to some extent the heat-load in the bodies of the insects. It is always surprising to find poisonous animals which do not have conspicuous, advertising coloration – most wasps and bees are yellow and black or red and black. Possibly food is in such short supply in the desert that not even poisonous insects can afford to be unnecessarily conspicuous.

While by no means as universal as a sandy colour, black is nevertheless surprisingly common among desert animals. Black is the ancestral colour of ravens, darkling beetles, and scarabs, and its presence in these groups is natural. But how can one explain the evolution of black wheatears, bee-flies and grasshoppers – forms whose relatives are never black in non-desert regions? Black is a conspicuous colour, especially in sandy regions. A black and yellow wasp may be conspicuous against a green leaf, but against a yellow background a totally black wasp is even more conspicuous.

In addition, the prevalence of black among desert animals may, in some instances, result from Müllerian mimicry, in which a number of different species, all possessing aposematic or warning attributes resemble one another and so become more easily recognized. Numerical losses are reduced in teaching predators to avoid a common warning colour and the adoption of a similar advertisement simplifies recognition. In Batesian mimicry, on the other hand, a relatively scarce, palatable and unprotected species, such as a black desert bee-fly resembles an abundant, relatively unpalatable or well-protected species such as a black desert bee and, on account of its disguise, is ignored by potential enemies. In nature, Batesian and Müllerian mimicry tend to merge into one another as model and mimic become relatively more or less distasteful.

Conspicuousness is not always associated with poisons, weapons or an unpleasant flavour. Some animals may be conspicuous for social reasons – so that the sexes may find one another easily, or that members of flocks and herds can keep together. The black and white desert wheatear is a wary bird, not easily approached by an enemy. It can afford to be black, because this does not endanger it to any degree, while its conspicuousness may confer some other advantage. It is not known whether it is distasteful or not.

Poisonous animals, armed with stings or fangs, are common in all but polar deserts. They include scorpions, centipedes, spiders, wasps, hornets, ants and venomous reptiles like vipers, cobras and

rattlesnakes. The only poisonous lizards, the gila monsters, are desert species found in the south-western United States of America. It is not always realized that most snakes are non-poisonous. In fact, only three groups are venomous: the back-fanged snakes; the deadly kraits, cobras and mambas; and the vipers and rattlesnakes, in which fang development attains its greatest perfection. It is questionable whether cobra or viper poison is the more lethal, for the physiological effects of the two types are quite different. Cobra venom is neurotoxic and induces paralysis; viper poison causes collapse and heart failure, depending upon the amount injected. Snake poisons contain a large number of toxic compounds and vary from one species to another. Viper poison usually contains an ingredient that causes clotting of the blood while cobra venom more often contains an anti-coagulant and, at the same time, causes breakdown of the red blood corpuscles.

Many poisonous serpents are highly conspicuous so that other animals are warned off and do not molest them. In desert regions, where food is scarce, the advantages of advertisement are probably outweighed by the disadvantage of being more readily spotted by a predator such as a secretary-bird or road-runner. The adaptive coloration of an animal is the result of a compromise between various conflicting influences.

Left: The Egyptian cobra is found from Morocco to Natal and extends into south-western Asia. It is probably the 'asp' with which Cleopatra committed suicide.

Below left: Scarab beetle rolling her ball of dung. Sacred to the sun god Ra of ancient Egypt, this is one of a number of desert dung beetles that scavenge on the droppings of domesticated animals in North Africa.

Below: Blue-tongued skink in threat display. This giant Australian skink measures over half a metre (about two feet) in length and shows well-marked behavioural temperature regulation.

Man and the Desert

Throughout his evolution, mankind has been intimately concerned with the desert. It seems probable that our ancestors evolved bipedal posture in woodland adjoining the semi-desert regions of Africa, and subsequently reduced much of the forest to savanna and desert. Indeed, as we shall see in this chapter, not only have desert conditions played an important role in the evolution of the human species, but man has subsequently reacted on his environment to enlarge very considerably the desert regions of the world. It is generally believed that after our pre-human ancestors had abandoned an arboreal life in the African rain forest, they became terrestrial hunters of the open sunny savanna. It was at this stage that humans assumed an upright posture, for they had already adopted bipedal locomotion. At that time, the regions of Africa that are now occupied by savanna – created largely as the result of human activities – were probably forested, and the forest would have extended to the edge of steppe grassland or desert. It seems probable, therefore, that man's first experience of open country may have been of semi-desert.

The desert and man's evolution

Man's upright posture is usually regarded as an adaptation, mainly for hunting, that freed the hands for the use of weapons and tools, and ensured the successful transition from an arboreal and herbivorous to a terrestrial and carnivorous mode of life. It is therefore argued that locomotion on two legs must be an adaptation for speed in open country that enabled our ancestors to chase and kill large game animals for food. If this were the case, however, it seems surprising that bipedal locomotion should not also have evolved

in baboons, which live mainly on the ground and are yet among the most successful of savanna monkeys. Many species of monkeys, as well as apes, will stand on their hind legs to obtain a clear view over tall grass and the like, and they may even take a few steps in this position, but they invariably revert to their four limbs whenever swift movement is required. Locomotion on two legs certainly leaves the hands free at all times, but it is not essential for the use of tools – angry chimpanzees, for example, will often use their hands to hurl sticks and stones at their adversaries. Monkeys and apes become adept at peeling fruit although they run on four limbs.

Bipedal mammals, other than man, such as kangaroos and jerboas, are certainly speedy creatures of deserts and open country, but they move by jumping and are balanced by their long tails. Their type of locomotion probably evolved from fast running on all fours. In its initial stages, human bipedal movement could not possibly have been fast enough either for evading the attacks of large predators or for chasing gazelles and antelopes. The suggestion has been made that throwing of missiles while running, only possible for creatures with stabilized bipedal locomotion, would have favoured the survival of man's ancestors who took to bipedalism. It seems doubtful, however, whether large animals could have been hunted successfully by primitive man until he had either domesticated the dog or become sufficiently gregarious to organize large-scale co-operative hunting parties. Primitive hunters in open country, such as the bushmen and Australian aborigines must stalk their prey, or else close in and use spears or clubs while the attention of the quarry is distracted by the attacks

Above: Botswana
bushman in the
Kalahari shooting
his poisoned arrow.
Bushmen are hunter-
gatherers. They are
magnificent archers
and can hit a moving
antelope at a range
of 130 metres or
more (over 400 feet).
Left: Bushman
making a fire to cook
his meal. Surplus
meat is cut into strips
and dried in the sun
to form 'biltong'.

have evolved while he was living at the forest's edge and making only brief excursions into the adjacent open country. Behind the cover of trees he could have stalked the grazing herbivores that ventured too close to the forest – an activity that would have facilitated an erect posture, for there is little undergrowth to provide cover beneath a dense canopy of trees. When in danger, he would immediately have pulled himself up into the branches of a tree.

The interdependence between movement on two legs and tool-making has long been recognized. With the successful development of both, ancestral man would have extended the range of his diet to include larger mammals. Previously, he must have depended for protein on eggs, insects, reptiles, young birds, baby mammals, rats, mice, or monkeys. He would also have scavenged on the prey of the larger carnivores. Indeed, it has been convincingly argued that man's ancestors were 'scavenge hunters', an occupation that requires neither particularly well-developed locomotory ability, nor camouflage. Later, thrown weapons were evolved from the tools used to assist in scavenging activities. The precursors of these weapons may well have been hurled from the cover of forest at animals grazing in semi-desert. This view somewhat contradicts earlier suggestions that man took to hunting when drought intensified the struggle for meat; and that the original function of tools was to remove skin and fur, and to divide flesh between the members of a group. Even if the earlier views were correct, however, it still implies that tools were probably developed in arid conditions.

Our ancestors presumably lost their covering of hair at about the same time that they acquired bipedal locomotion. This depilation cannot have been a direct response to climate because other mammals of tropical Africa have not, in general, lost their fur coats. (There is little evidence, either, for the suggestion that when man's ancestors left the forest, they went through a semi-aquatic stage during which they lived on the seashore and fed on molluscs and other littoral animals. In any case, by no means all marine mammals have lost their fur.)

The various hypotheses that have been proposed to explain the origins of man's hairlessness may be summarized as follows: adaptations to facilitate heat exchange, to conserve metabolic energy, to reduce the problem of ectoparasites, as the result of sexual selection, and as a result of a combination of selective pressures. Compared with the carnivores that existed in those days, or even with modern lions and leopards, man is inadequately equipped for hunting, and this must

of the hunters' dogs. It is thought that the capacity for walking on two legs is an adaptation for covering long distances, essential for efficient hunting. Even the arboreal chimpanzee can run faster than a man, however, and most monkeys can easily outdistance him, while baboons travel for long distances on their four legs.

During the 20 million years leading to the precursors of man from their arboreal ancestors, there was a gradual development in the use of tools, a gradual familiarization with the forest floor and, finally, an advance beyond the forest's edge. Until the end of the Pleistocene period, however, the area inhabited by humans would have been covered by forest, grading sharply into steppe and desert. It seems not improbable, therefore, that man's upright locomotion might

have placed a considerable strain on his physique. There would, therefore, have been a strong selection pressure to reduce overheating during the chase, even if it led to discomfort at night and in cool weather before clothing was invented or fires used to provide warmth. If, however, as suggested above, man's ancestors did not chase large mammalian prey, the hypothesis that hairlessness, combined with an efficient peripheral blood circulatory system, may have been an adaptation for cooling the body when our ancestors first became hunting carnivores, must also be questioned. Moreover, if hairlessness were an adaptation for hunting, one would have expected men to be less hairy than women.

Loss of hair, when coupled with the use of clothes, renders human beings extremely versatile and economical in their thermoregulation, in both tropical and temperate regions, but it seems certain that depilation must have taken place long before man had acquired the use of fire or clothing. The explanation of his hairlessness should be viewed in relation to inhabiting an environment at the border between forest and semi-desert grassland.

Diurnal and seasonal changes in temperature are very slight in tropical forest. Hairlessness,

therefore, would have imposed no great hardship on our ancestors while they were resting or gathering food among the trees, where the climate was constantly warm and damp. Any selective advantage of hairlessness must have been felt only during brief excursions into the steppe grassland and desert beyond. Here a reduction in thermal stress might have proved extremely beneficial, even if man the hunter did not rely on speed and endurance to the extent that has sometimes been supposed. The elephant and rhinoceros are comparatively hairless, yet they neither chase prey nor when adults are they hunted, except by man.

The human inhabitants of the tropics are usually dark-skinned, but the significance of this feature is by no means universally agreed. There is also some dispute as to whether a light or a dark skin is primitive in man. It seems probable that primitive man may have resembled modern Europeans and also the Australians and Ainu in having long shaggy hair and a beard. In this way he would have differed from the relatively hairless people now living in tropical Africa. The Negroes and other races with scanty beards and less hairy bodies must certainly have descended from hairier forms. A sparse beard on a naked body can only represent the loss of a full beard on a hairy

man; it cannot be an early stage of its evolution.

A dark skin absorbs more solar energy than a pale one and must, therefore, impose a greater heat-load. Yet the degree of skin pigmentation throughout the world is inversely proportional to latitude. The suggestion has therefore been made that pigment may protect the skin from ultraviolet radiation. A dose of ultra-violet light which damages pale skin to the extent of putting the sweat glands out of action has very little effect on moderately dark or tanned skin. Dark skins are especially characteristic of desert dwellers, and have probably been acquired independently by several different racial stocks, primarily as an adaptation to life in the tropical desert environment. Loss of pigmentation, on the other hand, probably evolved in temperate regions with a low intensity of sunlight, as an adaptation that enhances the synthesis of calciferol (vitamin D).

Man's primitive skin colour was most probably a pale brown. It seems unlikely that it could have been black, because the complex mechanism for flushing and blushing, if it has a function, would not have evolved in an animal whose pigment rendered it invisible. Flushing seems to have originated as a threat in males and as a courtship display among females. Charles Darwin knew that Negroes blush invisibly, but he merely concluded that this proved the mechanism to have no functional significance. Furthermore, there would have been no reason for black pigmentation to have evolved beneath coloured fur.

An apparent paradox exists in the suggestion that a pale brown skin may be primitive, and that the comparative hairiness of the Caucasian race is also a primate character. These facts can only be reconciled with man's undoubted tropical origin in the conclusion that the forerunners of the Caucasian peoples moved to temperate latitudes, the steppe lands of central Asia, and became depigmented, before they had evolved the degree of hairlessness found in other races of mankind.

Natural selection probably operates in many ways simultaneously, and its effects represent a compromise between a number of competing influences. It would be misleading to suggest that the diverse characters of modern man, except in a few specific instances, are the result of any single environmental factor. This chapter has been concerned with how the environmental conditions in which man's precursors evolved could have influenced his development in the ways that they have. The assumption that man arose as a speedy predator in open savanna does not appear

to be in any way justified. It would seem more likely that he began as an omnivorous scavenger at the forest's edge and later stalked his prey from the cover of the vegetation. Only when he became more gregarious, or had domesticated the dog, would he have been able to hunt large and speedy game animals in open country.

Desert created by man

The destruction of the African forest doubtless began when man first acquired the use of fire. This was probably well over 50,000 years ago for already between 50,000 and 60,000 years ago hearths were being used systematically by Acheulian peoples at lakeside sites by the Kilambo Falls, near the south-eastern corner of Lake Tanganyika. Fire is an essential tool in the shifting cultivation by which so much of the world's forest has been destroyed. Trees are felled and burned so that their ashes fertilize the ground. One or, perhaps, two good crops can be obtained from the clearing thus made before the soil loses its fertility. The process is then repeated elsewhere, and secondary forest takes the place of the original primary forest.

Secondary forest is poorer and contains less species than the original primary forest that it replaces. After many cycles, the forest disappears altogether and is replaced by wooded savanna, but the annual burning continues. Although fires must occur naturally from time to time, deliberate firing by man has a far greater effect on the vegetation. This is because man-made fires cover the same ground more frequently and, moreover, are not associated with thunderstorms. Natural fires, started by lightning, are frequently quenched by the rain that follows.

Fire does not usually spread continuously over whole tracts of vegetation. Normally small patches are burned and, later, neighbouring patches so that a mosaic pattern is produced. Some areas may be burned twice in a year while others escape from one year to the next. Fire favours perennial grasses with underground streams which regenerate rapidly and produce new green shoots, but it is always harmful to trees. Agriculture becomes unproductive and the land has to be utilized by grazing animals. As its quality degenerates, cattle have to be replaced by sheep and goats. Finally, only camels can survive when the forest has been reduced to desert.

All these stages can occur in a remarkably short period of time. Within living memory many areas of forest in Somalia, northern Uganda and

Above : A bush fire at Salamat, Chad. Fire plays a major role in the maintenance of savanna and has a marked effect on the nature of the vegetation.

Above : Bushmen have to be extremely economical with water which they store in gourds and ostrich shells.

men build temporary shelters of branches and grass. They keep no cattle, sheep or goats, but rely for their food on wild animals and plants. The men hunt with spears, clubs and bows: they are magnificent archers and can hit a moving antelope with a poisoned arrow at a range of 150 m (492 ft). The women and children dig the earth with grubbing sticks for edible bulbs and roots. They also collect *tsama* melons which are prized as a source of moisture. They obtain water from underground by sucking it up through a reed, and store it in ostrich shells and empty gourds. To reduce water-loss through sweating in hot weather, they urinate in pits dug in the ground and rest in the damp sand throughout the day. In times of plenty, bushmen are able to store fat in their protuberant buttocks, which gradually waste away during hungry periods. Shy, but intelligent and good-natured, they are extremely artistic and create beautiful rock paintings.

Like the bushmen, most of the Australian aborigines have now abandoned their ancient way of life. Only a few tribes, such as the Bindibu, still roam the deserts of the interior, where they hunt game with spear and boomerang, or gather edible roots and bulbs. These simple people enjoy a complex ritual life which helps them to survive in extremely primitive conditions. They believe that each clan or tribe is descended from a particular plant or animal which must be protected by magic ceremonies. They have an extremely sensitive physiological control of the blood that circulates in their skin, and are able to sleep naked at night without shivering, when the temperature is as low as 10°C (50°F). Their only shelter is a flimsy windbreak of sticks and grass; small fires, and the bodies of dogs provide the only warmth.

Only by adopting nomadic habits are human beings able to live permanently in areas where effective rain in any one place falls at intervals of several years. Until recently, the Tibbu of the Libyan desert wandered in small groups with a few goats across hundreds of miles of almost lifeless country where effective rain falls on the average only once between 30 and 50 years – except on a few isolated areas of high ground where the figure is reduced to between four and ten years. Nomadic tribes are found all over the Great Palaearctic desert. Some of them are small, with little social organization, while others are divided into clans with elaborate social, political and economic systems. They move within allotted territories, often defined by wells and springs.

The nomadic tribes of the Sahara and the deserts of western Asia travel on dromedaries, driving their herds of sheep and goats with them. Although they value horses greatly, these animals

western India have experienced all the stages from forest to desert. Climatic changes may play a part too, but man can not escape responsibility for having created much of the Sahara. In regions where the needs of the vegetation are delicately balanced by precarious rainfall, overgrazing and the cutting of the remaining trees for firewood can have a disastrous and irreversible effect.

Such effects are more conspicuous in some desert regions than in others, and are greatest where clay soils predominate. Perennial grasses are the first element of the vegetation to suffer from overgrazing. Their replacement by annual species is associated with a general reduction in the plant cover. Bare ground becomes flattened and compacted, so that it absorbs less rainwater than it would do if plants were present. The remainder runs off in gulleys and *wadis*, adding to the erosion that is already taking place.

Peoples of the desert

Despite their vast areas, deserts support less than five per cent of the world's population. Hunting and gathering was the original occupation of desert dwellers, but now only the bushmen of the Kalahari and the aborigines of the Australian desert pursue this difficult way of life. The bush-

are better suited to the cool deserts and steppes of central Asia where the bactrian camel replaces the dromedary. In distant ages, nomadic tribes of central Asia (such as the Huns and Mongols) developed the art of riding and fighting on horseback with lance or bow so effectively that, by the thirteenth century, they had become invincible.

The nomadic way of life is not necessarily backward although, as practised today, it may seem harsh and uncongenial to people accustomed to a sedentary existence.

Oases

Settled life is only possible in irrigated areas and oases. The various types of oases have been outlined in Chapter 3. The earliest civilization of Asia and Africa depended on the irrigation of fertile land along the valleys of great rivers such as the Tigris and Euphrates in Iraq, the Indus in Pakistan, Hwang-ho (China) and the Nile in Egypt. In South America early civilizations also depended on irrigation from the short rivers crossing the Atacama desert in Chile.

The oases of Asia and Africa have long and important histories. Their ecology has been so completely changed by human activities that it is difficult to reconstruct the original vegetation. In the Sahara and Arabian deserts the most important oasis crop is the date palm, in whose shade grow citrus fruits and other less hardy vegetables, often of high quality and with aromatic flavour or scents. These include figs, olives, apricots, pomegranates, guavas, wheat, maize, millet, lucerne, beans, peas, onions, tobacco, pimento tobacco and sweet potatoes. The date palm provides fruit for eating and the distillation of *aragi*, the stones are ground up to feed camels, the leaves are used as fuel and their fibres twisted into ropes or woven into a coarse cloth used to cover the wooden frames in which agricultural produce is transported. Finally, the trunks of dead palms are used for building houses, so that nothing is wasted.

Desert soils are often fertile because there has been no rain to wash away the nutrient that growing plants require. But the addition of irrigation water often leads to dissolved salts being drawn upwards through the soil, as a result of evaporation at its surface, and here they are deposited as an infertile crust. Salinization has plagued most areas of irrigation agriculture and is very difficult to overcome. The simplest way to remove unwanted salts is to wash them away with large amounts of fresh water, but this can only be done if there is good drainage. Irrigated fields

Above: Oasis of Tafilalt in the Ziz Valley, Morocco. Oases are among the most productive and densely cultivated regions in the world and, to some extent, reverse the worldwide tendency of deserts to expand.

have to be levelled for the distribution of water and this makes for poor drainage.

The inhabitants of most desert oases are engaged in continual strife against encroaching sand. Many North African oases have recently been enlarged by boring new wells, but the world's most extensively developed area of mined ground water is in western Texas. The isolation of oases affords protection from pests and diseases but, once introduced, both agricultural pests and human parasites find conditions very suitable for their increase. Oases are important not only on account of their own productivity, but because to some extent they reverse the worldwide tendency for deserts to increase as a result of over-exploitation and mismanagement of the land.

The future of the desert

The central problem of sustained land-use in arid regions is to maintain a balance between human requirements and the productivity of the land. Throughout the centuries, man has consistently been reducing the productive capability of arid lands by the over-exploitation of their resources. Rational exploitation of the desert complex must be based not on any single large-scale project, but on a multiplicity of smaller projects which complement one another.

Semi-arid and arid environments are only too

Below: An encampment of Rguibat Moors, one of the Berber peoples, in Morocco.

easily degraded into desert, but it is difficult and costly to reverse the process. Historically, man has mainly changed his methods of land-use to suit the changed conditions. From agriculture, he has switched to pastoralism, herding cattle and sheep until the vegetation and soil have become so impoverished that only goats and camels can survive: and, of all pastoral animals, the goat is chiefly responsible for enlarging the deserts of Africa and central Asia. By adding to the number of places at which livestock can secure water, the area of grazing can be widened, which helps to reduce the pressure around the original sources of water. This can be achieved by boring new wells and by constructing *haffirs* or artificial ponds in which seasonal rainwater can be stored. Such methods are effective, however, only so long as the herds are not permitted to increase.

If they do increase, the situation becomes worse, not better. This is what recently happened on the Sahel savanna region of Africa. By 1970, the land was supporting 24 million people and about the same number of cattle – roughly a third more people and twice as many animals as in 1930. The effect of providing more wells had been simply to make more pasture available thereby allowing greater multiplication of numbers. Consequently, when the inevitable period of drought came, its effect was all the more ferocious.

Thousands of starving cows clustered around the wells: indescribably emaciated, they would stagger away with bloated bellies to struggle from the churned mud at the water's edge, so that each bore-hole quickly became the centre of its own little desert of about 65 to 80 km (40 or 50 miles) square. Pastoralism is clearly a major cause of desert expansion and cannot, therefore, be advocated as a form of land-use in desert regions except under strict control and supervision.

Nevertheless, pastoral nomadism can be a remarkably efficient adaptation to the vagaries of the desert environments. The movements of the nomads are not random. In the Sahara, for instance, they move south during the dry seasons as far as they can go without entering the range of the tsetse-fly (which would infect their animals with the lethal cattle disease known as nagana). With the first rains, however, the grass springs up and the herds begin to move northwards until the edge of the desert is reached – when the southward journey begins again. This time, the cattle graze on the grass that grew up behind them on their northward journey and drink the standing water that remains from the rainy season. Back in their dry season area, they find a crop of grass and stubble that will have to last them throughout eight or nine months of drought until the rains come again. In desert regions where the climate is even more extreme than in the Sahelian zone of Africa, nomadism is the only way of life by which man can survive, except in oases.

The nomadic tribes are found all over the Sahara and include the Tibbu, the Tuareg, Teda, and Beja. Although the nomadic way of life is probably the only one which will ever produce much in the way of food from arid desert regions, governmental policies towards nomadism are usually unimaginative and unenlightened. They appear to be directed chiefly towards the settlement of the nomads and the restriction of their migration routes. If traditional nomadism were to disappear, however, vast areas that are now productive would become permanently useless to mankind. It would surely be better, therefore, to encourage and modernize the nomadic way of life. The hardship that nomadic people endure could be ameliorated by a flying-doctor service, mobile markets and educational facilities. Grazing could be controlled and even improved, news of distant rainfall transmitted by radio, and so on. In this way, the desert cores might continue to contribute usefully to the economy of man provided, of course, that they were not over-exploited.

Another way in which desert and semi-desert could be utilized in the service of mankind, without further destruction of the habitat, is by game ranching. Wild game are so much more mobile than domesticated animals that they do not normally cause overgrazing and soil erosion. Although the saiga antelope was almost exterminated during the nineteenth century, it was accorded complete protection by the Russian government in 1919. The population subsequently increased from about 1000 animals in 1930 to over 2,500,000 in 1960. Since 1950, saiga antelope have been cropped and, today, about 350,000 are killed annually to provide 6700 tonnes (6600 tons) of meat and 24,000 square metres (28,700 sq yds) of leather. In addition to true desert animals, such as oryx and addax antelope, many of the East African species are well adapted to heat and drought. They include the black rhinoceros, wild ass, eland and ostrich, which might profitably be reintroduced into the savanna belts on the desert's fringe. When their populations had increased they could be culled, like the saiga antelope, to provide food without detriment to the environment. The main problem presented by this type of land-use is that the great mobility of such animals makes them difficult to control, or to protect from poachers.

A certain amount of semi-desert country can be farmed without irrigation, provided that the land is left fallow for some 15 or 20 years before it is cropped again. Millet and sorghum, grown in this way, can provide food without harming the land. When cash-crops are introduced to earn foreign exchange, however, fertility declines because ecologically fragile regions cannot take the strain of intensive agriculture.

Irrigation schemes are effective when water is obtainable in quantity from regions beyond the desert's fringe. Where the water is a fossil resource which is not being recharged, however, the level of the water-table drops steadily and the land will inevitably revert to desert. This is probably the case in many parts of the Sahara, including much of Libya and Algeria, as well as in most of the Great American desert, including Baja California, where short-term farming projects are based on wells with an expectancy of, at most, 10 to 15 years' production.

Economy of water is vital for efficient agriculture in deserts, and the traditional agricultural methods used by oasis dwellers, developed over a long period of time, are by no means uneconomical. Even more efficient use of existing water can be made through hydroponic cultivation. Nutrient solutions, pumped once or twice daily through plastic pipes perforated by small holes, irrigate plant roots growing in *erg* sand without wetting the surface of the soil, so that little water is wasted through evaporation. In this way, the amount of

Right: A Tuareg, a member of the largest of the nomadic Berber tribes in the Sahara who exchange surplus meat for the items for which they are not self-sufficient, such as tea.

Left: The face of the desert is changing rapidly in areas such as parts of Algeria, shown here, where oil and gas can be obtained.

Above: Desert expansion can be checked even by small-scale activities. Here rock walls check rapid run-off of water in the Namib desert.

water required to grow tomatoes, for example, may be more than halved.

The water which percolates underground inevitably dissolves minerals from rocks and sediments on its way. Consequently, when it emerges from springs and bore-holes, it is often highly mineralized. Although desalination is still too expensive to produce water for agricultural purposes, even sea-water can be desalinized cheaply enough to provide water for livestock.

Soil erosion can be checked in a number of ways, and dunes stabilized by spraying them with a mixture of oil and synthetic rubber before planting seedlings of acacia or eucalyptus, which can grow in areas where the rainfall is as low as 150 mm (6 ins) per year. Considerable success is being achieved in the semi-arid Argentine pampas, where *erg* can be converted to grassland within three months. The procedure is complicated and expensive, however.

The most obvious and coveted riches of the world's desert wastelands are the deposits of oil and minerals that lie underground. In addition, the tropical deserts possess an inexhaustible supply of solar energy. This can already be harnessed for research and domestic purposes and may, one day, provide unlimited power for industrial development. Industrial economy uses very much less water per head of population than does agriculture or stock-rearing. The day may even come, therefore, when industry is developed in the desert countries of the world while the industrial countries of today concentrate more on the agriculture for which they are climatically better suited.

The problems of arid lands are complex and there is no single solution to them. But the more ways in which a region can be rationally exploited at the same time, the less will this exploitation harm the environment. Desert expansion is merely one of many consequences of the world's current population explosion and it is no use attempting to deal with it in isolation. It is but part of a graver threat to the continued existence of our species.

Under the pressures of modern society, man often tires of crowded cities, and longs for the wide open spaces. Air transport places the world at his doorstep, so that the amenity and tourist value of the wilderness may eventually even exceed that of its mineral wealth and agricultural potential. When that day comes, the conservation of the natural flora and fauna will have been justified, whatever its cost.

Glossary

Acheulian people The hunter-gatherers whose hand-axe culture succeeded the pebble-tool culture of the earlier ape men.

Aestivation Dormancy during the hot, dry summer season.

Archaean Of the earliest geological period, that is Pre-Cambrian.

Artesian well A well producing a constant supply of water rising spontaneously to the surface because it has been sunk into a permeable stratum that has impervious strata above and below it. The hydrostatic pressure of the water in the permeable stratum is sufficient to expel it from the ground.

Arthropod A member of the largest phylum (division) in the animal kingdom. Its members have a hard, jointed external skeleton, and include crustaceans, insects and arachnids.

Bajada An almost continuous cover of gravels formed by the coalescence of alluvial fans at the mouths of valleys.

Barchan A crescent-shaped dune, widely characteristic of the Arabian, Asian and American deserts, but comparatively rare in the Sahara. Barchans are usually found where the supply of sand is intermittent. They are highly mobile, with gentle windward and steep leeward slopes, and may attain great size. The horns move ahead of the main mass of the dune.

'Basement complex' Pre-Cambrian sedimentary rock underlying much of the Sahara.

Bedrock Underlying rock structure which becomes weathered to form soil.

'Berg' wind The dry, easterly wind from the interior of Africa, characteristic of the Namib desert.

Biome Any major geographical region having a characteristic flora and fauna.

'Block tectonics' Movement of large blocks of the earth's crust.

Bulbil Small bulb formed from a larger bulb as a form of vegetative reproduction.

Cambrian period The earliest fossil-bearing geological period, lasting from about 510 to 430 million years ago.

Carboniferous period The geological period during which the coal measures were deposited, lasting from about 260 to 200 million years ago.

Carnivore An animal that feeds on the flesh of other animals.

Chott Salt marsh of Algeria and Tunisia, often covered with a thin film of salt or dry sand, where water from artesian sources evaporates. *See also* playa, sebkha.

Cold desert Desert having a hot summer and cold winter, such as the Gobi or Great Basin deserts.

Colocynth Gourd plant (similar to cucumber) with bitter, purgative fruit.

Coniferous forest Forest of cone-bearing trees such as pine, spruce and larch, characteristic of cooler latitudes, that do not shed their leaves in

winter. *See also* deciduous.

Crepuscular Active in twilight, at dawn and dusk.

Cretaceous period The last geological period of the Mesozoic era (the age of the great reptiles) lasting from about 130 to 60 million years ago.

Crustacean Large class of animals with hard integuments; mostly aquatic, such as crabs, lobsters and shrimps. Terrestrial examples include woodlice or slaters.

Cryptic coloration Coloration of animals that conceals them by its resemblance to that of their environment.

Crystalline rock Igneous rock derived from the interior of the earth, often containing a large proportion of quartz.

Deciduous forest Forest of trees that shed their leaves at certain seasons, usually autumn. *See also* evergreen or coniferous forest.

Devonian period The geological period, during much of which desert conditions prevailed, which lasted from about 310 to 260 million years ago.

Digitigrade An animal that walks on the ventral surface of the toes, not on the whole foot: locomotion characteristic of cats and dogs.

Diurnal Daily, or occurring during the daytime.

Ecology Study of the relations of plants and animals to their surroundings, both living and non-living.

Ephemeral Short-lived plant that completes its life-cycle within a few days.

Euphorbia Plant belonging to a family many of whose members are succulent, and characteristic of Old World deserts.

Filter feeding A form of feeding used by aquatic organisms that filter small edible particles from the water in which they live.

Gallinaceous bird Bird of the same family as grouse, ptarmigan and capercaillie.

Geomorphology The study of the formation of the earth's surface.

Great Palaearctic desert The huge desert region of Africa and Asia including the Sahara, Arabian, Iranian, Thar, Kyzyl Kum, Kara Kum, Takla Makan and Gobi deserts.

Hammada Rocky pavement of eroded bedrock from which most of the desert soil has been removed.

Herbivore An animal that feeds on plants.

Hibernation Winter dormancy during which metabolism is slowed down. The body temperature of hibernating mammals drops to that of the surroundings.

Hydroponics The cultivation of plants by allowing their roots to spread in an inert material such as quartz sand which is irrigated with a nutrient solution.

Icheumon A parasitic wasp that lays its eggs in the larvae or eggs of other insects or spiders.

Igneous rock Rock formed by the solidification of

molten fluids injected into the earth's crust or extruded onto its surface from the interior.

Iguanid A lizard of the American family Iguanidae.

Inflorescence Flowering shoot.

Insolation Exposure to the rays of the sun.

Integument Outer covering of tissue, for example, skin, or the cuticle of arthropods.

Interglacial period A period of milder climate between two ice ages.

Lacertid A lizard of the Old World family Lacertidae.

Loess Clay consisting of fine rock-flour originating in arid regions and transported by wind.

Macro-environment The large-scale environment of an animal or plant, as opposed the micro-environment immediately surrounding it.

Marsupial Mammal in which the young develops inside the uterus of the mother but is born in a very undeveloped state and is sheltered in a marsupial pouch; for example, kangaroos and opossums.

Micro-environment The environment immediately surrounding a plant or animal.

Morphology The study of form, especially that of the outer form, inner structure and development of living organisms and their parts.

Nefud Sand-dune field of the Arabian desert, for example.

Nocturnal Active at night.

Oasis Fertile spot in the desert where plants grow because there is water.

Pedipalps Second paired appendage of arachnids which may bear claws as in scorpions or have a sensory function. In male spiders they are used in mating.

Permafrost Layer of tundra soil that is permanently frozen because only the surface melts in the short summer.

Photosynthesis The formation by green plants of organic compounds from carbon dioxide and water using energy absorbed from sunlight.

Physiology The study of the processes that take place within living organisms.

Playa Alluvial plain in western America in which temporary saline lakes may form. *See also* chott and sebkha.

Pleistocene epoch The geological period lasting from approximately one million to 10,000 years ago, during which four ice ages occurred.

Pliocene epoch The geological period lasting from about 12 to 1 million years ago.

Polar desert The region surrounding the poles in which few plants grow because the water is frozen.

Pre-Cambrian Sedimentary rock laid down before the Cambrian period.

Quiescence State of inactivity, which is often a response to unfavourable temperatures.

Rain-forest Luxurious forest of the equatorial and wet tropical regions of the world.

Reg Stony desert with a mosaic surface of gravel in the western Sahara. *See also* serir.

Rhizome Underground stem bearing bulbs in the axils of reduced leaves, which serve as a means of vegetative reproduction.

Savanna Tropical woodland and grassland biome lying between rain-forest and desert.

Scree Mass of rock fragments at foot of hill or mountain resulting from frost action or insolation.

Sebkha Enclosed basin covered by saline crust in Libya. *See also* chott and playa.

Seif dune Longitudinal sand-dune caused by the wind blowing in a constant direction, which moves fine and coarse sand leaving deep troughs parallel to the path of the wind.

Serir Stony desert with a mosaic surface of gravel in Libya and Egypt. *See also* reg.

Silurian period The geological period lasting from approximately 350 to 310 million years ago.

Solar heat The heat of the sun.

Sphagnum The type of moss that grows in bogs forming peat.

Stellar dune Star-shaped dune caused by wind blowing at different times from all directions.

Steppe Level, grassy, treeless plain extending over great distances.

Subtropical desert Desert lying outside the tropics and which may have a hot summer but a cold winter.

Succulent A type of xerophytic plant that stores water within its tissues so that it has a fleshy appearance, for example, cacti and many euphorbias.

Taiga Biome of evergreen coniferous forest which is characterized by short, cool summers and intensely cold winters.

Temperate forest Forest biome in temperate regions lying between steppe grassland and taiga.

Thermoregulation Regulation of body temperature.

Transverse dune Sand-dune resulting from moderate, one-directional winds moving only light sand.

Tropical desert Desert lying within the tropics and which therefore enjoys hot summers and comparatively warm winters. *See also* cold desert.

Tundra Biome lying between taiga and polar snowlands where only a little soil melts in summer above the permafrost, so that trees cannot grow. The winters are more intensely cold than those of the taiga.

Tympanic bulla Bony projection of the skull protecting and enclosing the middle ear.

Ungulate A hoofed mammal which is usually adapted for life in open country. There are two distinct groups: odd-toed ungulates such as horses, tapirs and rhinoceroses; and even-toed ungulates including pigs, deer, cattle, hippopotamuses and camels.

Vertebrate Any animal with a skeleton of cartilage or bone, and a skull enclosing the brain; for example, fish, amphibians, reptiles, birds and mammals.

Viviparous snake A snake that bears living young, developing from eggs that hatch within the body of the mother.

Wadi Desert watercourse which is dry most of the time but which carries off the rain from sporadic thunderstorms.

Xerophytic Able to endure conditions of drought.

Bibliography

BODENHEIMER, F. S. *Animal Life in Palestine* (Mayer, Jerusalem 1935)

BRIGGS, L. C. *Tribes of the Sahara* (Harvard University Press, Cambridge, Mass. 1960)

BROWN, G. W. (Ed) *Desert Biology*, 2 volumes, (Academic Press, New York 1968, 1974)

BUXTON, P. A. *Animal Life in Deserts* (Arnold, London 1955)

CLOUDSLEY-THOMPSON, J. L. (Ed) *Biology of Deserts* (Institute of Biology, London 1954)

CLOUDSLEY-THOMPSON, J. L. *Desert Life* (Aldus, London 1974)

CLOUDSLEY-THOMPSON, J. L. *Desert Life* (Pergamon Press, Oxford 1965)

CLOUDSLEY-THOMPSON, J. L. *The Ecology of Oases* (Merrow, Watford 1974)

CLOUDSLEY-THOMPSON, J. L. *Terrestrial Environments* (Croom Helm, London 1975)

CLOUDSLEY-THOMPSON, J. L. *The Zoology of Tropical Africa* (Weidenfeld & Nicolson, London 1969)

CLOUDSLEY-THOMPSON, J. L. & CHADWICK, M. J. *Life in Deserts* (Foulis, London 1964)

DREGNE, H. E. (Ed) *Arid Land in Transition* (American Association for the Advancement of Science, Washington D.C. 1971)

HADLEY, N. F. *Environmental Physiology of Desert Organisms* (Halsted Press, New York 1975)

HAVILAND, M. D. *Forest, Steppe and Tundra* (Cambridge University Press, 1926)

HILLS, E. S. *Arid Lands: A Geographical Appraisal* (Methuen, London 1966; UNESCO, Paris 1966)

KIRMIZ, J. P. *Adaptation to Desert Environment* (Butterworth, London 1962)

LEOPOLD, A. S. *The Desert* (Life Nature Library, New York 1962)

McGINNIES, W. M. (Ed) *Deserts of the World* (University of Arizona Press, Tucson 1968)

McGINNIES, W. M. *Food, Fiber and the Arid Lands* (University of Arizona Press, Tucson 1971)

SCHMIDT-NIELSEN, K. *Desert Animals: Physiological Problems of Heat and Water* (Oxford University Press, 1964)

SMILEY, T. L. & ZUMBERGE J. H. (Eds) *Polar Deserts and Modern Man* (University of Arizona Press, Tucson 1974)

WALTON, K. *The Arid Zones* (Hutchinson University Library, London 1969)

Index

Acknowledgements

We are grateful to the following for permission to reproduce photographs on pages:

Frontispiece Marka; 6 Nino Cirani; 9(top) Marka; 9(bottom) Explorer/Suinot; 11 Giorgio Gualco; 12 Giorgio Gualco; 14 Giorgio Gualco; 16 Nino Cirani; 16–17 Nino Cirani; 17 Australian Information Service; 20(top) Marka; 20(bottom) P2; 21 Explorer/Jacques Trotignon; 22–23 Marka/Norman Myers; 24 Explorer/P. Forge; 25 Explorer/P. Verbeck; 26 Explorer/Suinot; 27(top) Giorgio Gualco; 27(bottom) Explorer/Fabins Henrion; 28 (top) Giorgio Gualco; 28(bottom) Explorer/P. Verbeck; 29 Marka/Dondero; 30 Nino Cirani; 32 Marka; 34 Erik Hosking; 35 Giorgio Gualco; 36(top) Explorer/S. Bougaeff; 36(bottom) Jacana; 37 Jacana; 38 Marka; 39 Jacana; 40 Bruce Coleman; 41(top) Jacana; 41(bottom) Jacana; 42–43(top) Jacana/P. Massart; 42(bottom) Jacana; 43(bottom) Jacana; 44 Photo Researchers/Rychetnik; 45(top) Jacana; 45(middle) Bruce Coleman/Jane Burton; 45(bottom) Bruce Coleman/Jane Burton; 47 Jacana; 48(top) Jacana; 48(bottom) Jacana; 49 Marka; 50 Jacana; 51 Jacana; 52(left) Marka/RHO; 52–53 Marka; 53(bottom) Marka; 54 Nino Cirani; 56–57 P2; 58 Jacana; 59 Marka; 60–61 Explorer/P. Forge; 61(top) Marka; 62 Explorer; 63 Folco Quilici; 64 (top) Marka; 64(bottom) Jacana; 65 Nino Cirani; 66 Nino Cirani; 67 Nino Cirani; 68 Bruce Coleman/ J. & D. Bartlett; 70(top) Marka/Norman Myers; 70(bottom) Jacana/Michel Bailleau; 71 Marka/Bavaria Verlag; 72–73 Marka/Bavaria Verlag; 74–75 Nino Cirani; 75(right) Jacana/J. Prevost; 76 Marka; 77(top) Giorgio Gualco; 77(bottom) Explorer/Jacques Trotignon; 79 Bruce Coleman/S. C. Bisserot; 80 Jacana; 81 Jacana; 82 (top) Jacana/C & M Motton; 82(middle) Bruce Coleman/Jane Burton; 82(bottom) Ardea/J. L. Mason; 83 Bruce Coleman/Jane Burton; 84 Jacana; 85(left) Bruce Coleman/Jane Burton; 85(right) Bruce Coleman/Jane Burton; 86 Bruce Coleman/Norman Myers; 87(top) Jacana/A. R. Devez; 87(bottom) Jacana/Gillon; 88(top) Ardea/Beste; 88(bottom) Bruce Coleman/Lee Lyon; 89 Bruce Coleman; 90(top) Marka/Hal Kanzler; 90(bottom) Jacana/Fievet; 91 Jacana/J. L. S. Dubois; 92 Jacana/Serge Yoff; 93 Ardea; 94 Jacana; 96(left) Jacana/Robert; 96–97 Jacana/Renaud; 97(right) Jacana/Trotignon; 98 Bruce Coleman/Dan Freeman; 99 Novosti; 100–101 Bruce Coleman/ Moira & Rod Burland; 101(right) Marka; 102 Marka/Marc Lelo; 103 Jacana/J. Robert; 104 Bruce Coleman/James Simon; 106 Bruce Coleman/Jane Burton; 107 Jacana/Fievet; 108(bottom) Ardea; 108–9 Jacana/ Dubois; 109 Bruce Coleman; 110 Nino Cirani; 112 Marka; 113 Marka; 114 Marka; 115 Marka; 116 Explorer; 117 Dr Lino Pellegrini; 118 Nino Cirani; 119 Explorer; 121 Explorer; 122 Nino Cirani; 123 Marka.